DISCOVERY

PIRATES

Philip Steele

Consultant: David Cordingly

T0124337

Published by Anness Publishing Ltd, Blaby Road,
Wigston, Leicestershire LE18 4SE
Email: info@anness.com

Web: www.annesspublishing.com

Anness Publishing has a new picture agency outlet for
images for publishing, promotions or advertising.
Please visit our website www.practicalpictures.com for
more information.

Publisher: Joanna Lorenz
Managing Editor, Children's Books: Sue Grabham
Senior Editor: Gilly Cameron Cooper
Editorial Reader: Joy Wotton
Series Design: John Jamieson
Designer: Margaret Sadler
Illustration: Donato Spedaliere
Colour work: Clive Spong, Linden Artists
Picture Research: Charlotte Lippmann
Photography: John Freeman
Stylist: Melanie Williams

Trees are being cultivated to replace the materials used
to make this product. For further information about
our ecological investment scheme, go to
www.annesspublishing.com/trees

© Anness Publishing Limited 2011

A CIP catalogue record for this book is available from
the British Library

Anness Publishing would like to thank the following
children, and their parents, for modelling for this book:
Harriet Bartholomew, Winnie Collate, Joe Davis,
Sun-Kiet Hoang, Erin McCarthy, Armani McKenzie,
Noura Mehdinejad, Goke Omoleua, Diana Sousa, Tom
Swaine-Jameson

PICTURE CREDITS
Ancient Art and Architecture Collection Ltd: 4cr, 5br,
10cr, 20br, 43bl, 50bl, 51tl, 55tr; Bridgeman Art
Library: 16bl, 22bl, 23tr, 47b, 55br, 58br; English
Heritage: 48b; E.T. Archive: 5br, 9b, 29tl, 37t, 44bl;
Mary Evans Picture Library: 8c, 10b, 14bl, 18bl, 25bl,
29cl, 30bl, 37br, 40br, 41tl, 41bl, 43tr, 51bl, 51br;
Falmouth Museum: 12bl; The Fotomas Index: 11tr,
17br, 17bl, 28tr, 28cl, 36cr, 39tl, 57bl; Sonia
Halliday Photographs: 46t; Robert Harding
Picture Library: 13tr; Michael Holford
Photographs: 8tr; Katz Pictures Ltd: 10tr, 41r;
Museum of London: 43tl, 46c; National
Maritime Museum: 9tr, 12tl, 17tr, 20c,
38bl, 39tr, 42t, 46br, 47tl, 51tr, 54t,
56br, 57cr; Peter Newark's Historical
Pictures: 5t, 13tr, 16tl, 17tl, 24b, 25t,
25c, 25br, 36cl; Universitetets
Oldsaksamling: 50tr; Parker Library,
Corpus Christi College, Cambridge: 8b,
58c; Ann Ronan at Image Select: 4cl, 21tl, 21br,
42bl; York Archaeological Trust: 40tr.

PUBLISHER'S NOTE
Although the advice and information in this book
are believed to be accurate and true at the time of
going to press, neither the authors nor the publisher
can accept any legal responsibility or liability for any
errors or omissions that may have been made nor for
any inaccuracies nor for any loss, harm or injury that
comes about from following instructions or advice in
this book.

☠ CONTENTS ☠

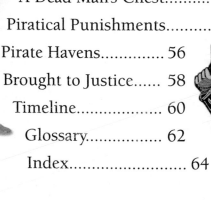

Death on the Horizon

Imagine a scene about 400 years ago. A Spanish treasure ship is homeward bound from the port of Cartagena in South America. It is loaded with chests of gold, silver and precious gems captured from the former Aztec empire. The wind is set fair. The sailor on lookout duty rubs his eyes. Is that a cloud on the horizon or a distant sail? Two hours later, the deck is soaked in blood and the ship is adrift and burning, a victim of piracy. The treasure will never reach the Spanish king.

Piracy means robbery at sea. It can still happen today, but until steam power replaced sail in the 1860s, ships were slow and heavy to manoeuvre, making them more vulnerable to attack. Many coasts were uncharted, and pirate ships could hide among remote creeks and islands, beyond the reach of the law. Piracy is as old as the history of shipping – the word itself comes from the ancient Greek word for attack. Pirates have also been called corsairs, buccaneers, freebooters, rovers, sea beggars and filibusters.

▲ DANGER AHEAD

A merchant seaman lookout watches a ship through his spyglass. There are suspiciously few crew on deck, and they are wearing an odd assortment of clothes. A bogus national flag has been replaced with the menacing skull and crossbones. It is a pirate ship.

CORSAIR ATTACK ▶
Dragut Rais was a corsair from the Barbary Coast of North Africa. The coast between Algiers and Tripoli was the scene of devastating Muslim attacks on ships from the Christian countries of the Mediterranean. Running warfare between the two faiths lasted from the 1500s to the 1800s. Dragut, a former slave of the Christians, became one of the greatest corsair commanders. He was killed at the Siege of Malta in 1565.

▲ PIRATE OR HERO?

The English seafarer Francis Drake is knighted by Queen Elizabeth I in 1581. Drake had just returned from a voyage during which he raided Spanish colonies and shipping. His loot may have been £500,000 – about £70 million at today's values. To the English, Drake was a hero. To the Spanish, he was a common pirate. Many empire-building countries encouraged their seamen to attack ships of other nations.

◀ THE CRUEL BUCCANEER
In the late 1660s, the Frenchman François l'Olonnois organized buccaneers (outlaws of the Caribbean) into pirate armies. At first the buccaneers had lived by hunting on Hispaniola and other islands, but they gradually turned to piracy. L'Olonnois was notorious for torturing his enemies. When he himself was taken prisoner by native warriors in Central America, his captors tore his body apart and burned it.

◀ DEATH OF A PIRATE

Edward Teach (otherwise known as Blackbeard) was the terror of North American waters until his violent death in 1718. His pirate ship *Adventure* was attacked by a British naval sloop under Lieutenant Robert Maynard. In a ferocious hand-to-hand battle in Ocracoke Inlet, North Carolina, Blackbeard was shot five times and received 20 sword wounds before he died. His head was hacked off and tied to the bowsprit of Maynard's ship, like a ghoulish figurehead.

◀ PIRATES ON BOARD!

An officer is at the pirates' mercy, and the crew is overpowered. The sailors might be given the choice of joining the pirates or being set adrift in a small boat. The pirates probably robbed any passengers, and then seized the whole ship, or just its supplies or the cargo.

A MODEL PRIVATEER ▶

Ships with a variety of different sails, like the model brig (*right*) and topsail schooners, were fast and manoeuvrable. This made them favourites with the pirates and privateers of the 1700s and 1800s. Privateers were captains who had been given legal authority to raid the merchant shipping of an enemy country. The ships of these official pirates were also called privateers. The line between privateering and piracy was often a very thin one.

The Seven Seas

Merchant ships have crossed the world's oceans for thousands of years. In the days of sail, the pattern of world trade was determined by the winds and currents, by reefs and straits, and by islands where fresh drinking water could be taken on board. Shipping had little choice but to follow certain routes. These routes attracted pirates, like a carcass attracts hungry vultures.

By the 1690s, pirates were sailing halfway across the world in search of plunder. A common route for them became known as "the Pirate Round". It went from the Caribbean islands to West Africa, south around the Cape of Good Hope to Madagascar and the Indian Ocean, and then all the way back across the Atlantic to North America. As sea faring nations began to organise anti-piracy patrols, pirates became hemmed in, restricted to the Caribbean or the South China Sea until no hiding place was safe for them.

GREENLAND

NORTH AMERICA

New York

COLONIAL AMERICA

New Orleans
Gulf of Mexico   Nassau
BAHAMAS
Vera Cruz   CUBA   PUERTO RICO
JAMAICA   HISPANIOLA
Caribbean Sea
Portobello
Nombre de Dios   THE SPANISH MAIN
Panama City   Cartagena

Atlantic Ocean

Pacific Ocean

N

SOUTH AMERICA

Cape Horn

◀ ROVING THE OCEANS
In the early 1700s, a pirate captain would readily sail tens of thousands of kilometres in search of his victims. Ships would be stolen, sunk, exchanged or wrecked on the way. A single voyage could take several years.

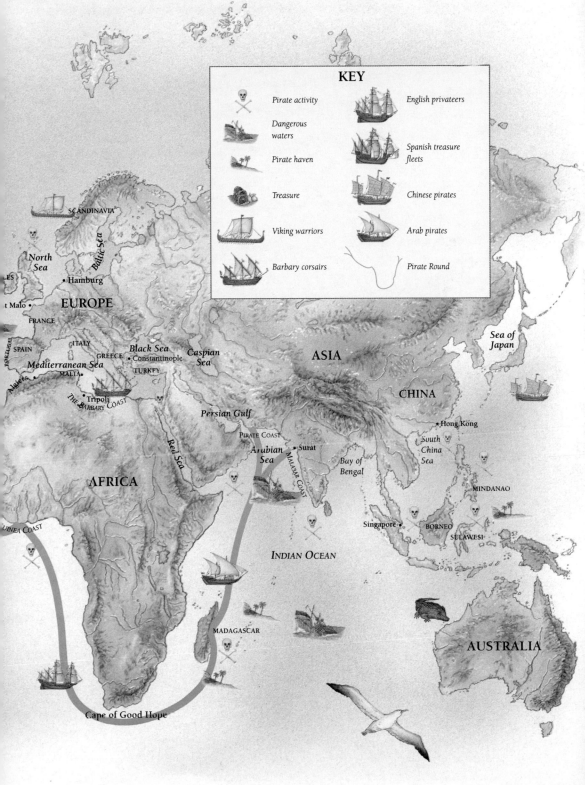

KEY

Pirate activity		English privateers	
Dangerous waters		Spanish treasure fleets	
Pirate haven		Chinese pirates	
Treasure		Arab pirates	
Viking warriors		Pirate Round	
Barbary corsairs			

SCANDINAVIA

Baltic Sea

North Sea

• Hamburg

EUROPE

FRANCE

t Malo

ES

SPAIN

PORTUGAL

ITALY

GREECE

Mediterranean Sea

Algiers•

MALTA•

THE BARBARY COAST

Tripoli•

Black Sea

• Constantinople

TURKEY

Caspian Sea

ASIA

CHINA

Sea of Japan

Persian Gulf

Red Sea

PIRATE COAST

Arabian Sea

• Surat

MALABAR COAST

Bay of Bengal

• Hong Kong

South China Sea

AFRICA

UINEA COAST

INDIAN OCEAN

Singapore •

BORNEO

MINDANAO

SULAWESI

MADAGASCAR

AUSTRALIA

Cape of Good Hope

Pirates through the Ages

Greek pirates were robbing Phoenician and Assyrian trading ships in the Mediterranean Sea at least as far back as 735BC. Nearly four centuries later, piracy was a major problem for the Macedonian ruler Alexander the Great, and remained a threat during the Roman Empire. In the 1st century AD, at the peak of the Roman Empire, a 1,000-ship pirate force destroyed an entire Roman fleet and plundered hundreds of villages along the southern coast of what is now Turkey.

During the Middle Ages, local pirates preyed on shipping along the coasts of the British Isles and the northern shores of France and Germany. In the 1400s and 1500s, European nations sailed the world in search of riches and new lands. They plundered and enslaved the peoples they conquered and then began to raid each other's ships. Piracy reached its peak on the Spanish Main (the coasts of the Caribbean and Central and South America) during the 1700s. It was still a common threat in the South China Sea in the 1920s.

▲ ANCIENT BATTLES

A Phoenician merchant vessel bound for an Assyrian port needed to be heavily armed. The ancient empire of Assyria stretched from the Mediterranean Sea to the Persian Gulf. Both of these coastlines were plagued by pirates, particularly from Greece. In 694BC, an Assyrian ruler called Sennacherib declared war on the pirates of the Gulf Coast. Even so, it remained a centre of piracy for most of the following 2,500 years because of the busy trading ship traffic.

SEA WOLVES ▶

Vikings were ferocious Scandinavian warriors who sailed in search of land, slaves and treasure. Their name originally meant pirates or raiders. Raiding parties attacked the British coast from AD789. During the following century the Vikings became feared all over Europe. They fought their way down the rivers of eastern Europe and traded in Russia and the Middle East. They sailed westwards to Iceland, Greenland and the coasts of North America. Viking warriors fought with axes and swords, and were said to bite their shields in the frenzy of battle.

◀ A MURDEROUS MONK

The year is 1217 and a Flemish pirate is beheaded during a brutal sea battle off the coast of south-east England. The pirate is Eustace, a one-time monk turned murderer. Eustace, who hired out his privateering services to both English and French fleets, was much feared as a sorcerer and believed to be in league with the Devil.

◄ SMOKING DREADLOCKS!

Edward Teach (or Blackbeard) was a blustering, bullying giant of a man. He terrified his victims by tying smouldering lengths of cord soaked in gunpowder in his long, knotted hair. By 1716, there was so much piracy in the Caribbean that pirates such as Blackbeard sought new hunting grounds. The British colonies in North America provided rich pickings, with the help of corrupt officials who pocketed a share of the plunder.

▲ BROTHERS IN ARMS

Aruj and Kheir-ed-din were the most feared corsairs of the Barbary Coast in the early 1500s. They were given the nickname Barbarossa, which means red-bearded. The brothers were condemned by their Spanish and Italian victims as cruel pirates. In reality they were brilliant naval commanders and respected political leaders, who became part of the wider conflict between Islamic and Christian states.

◄ SOUTH CHINA SEAS

A British naval force sails into Bias Bay, a notorious pirate stronghold to the east of Hong Kong, in September 1849. The bay was the base of Cui A-Bao, the lieutenant of a fearsome pirate commander called Shi Wu-Zai. The British ships blasted Cui A-Bao's pirate fleet out of the water and over 400 pirates were killed. Two years later, Cui was captured, and killed himself rather than face banishment. The islands of the Far East, from China to the Philippines, were infested with pirates for thousands of years. Coastal villages were targeted as well as merchant ships.

Becoming a Pirate

I n the 1700s, if you became a pirate, it was called "going on the account". Why did people do it? For some, it was an escape from a life of hardship and poverty. Slaves, such as the Africans taken by force to the Caribbean in the 1600s and 1700s, had nothing to lose. Some pirates were political rebels, rather like today's hijackers or terrorists. Many were regular sailors, who had been captured and forced to join up with the pirates. Others were gamblers and adventurers, who found everyday life boring or could not stand polite society. Some were respected figures, such as lords, ladies or wealthy merchants, who rejected the society they were part of. Craftily, they hired others to do the dirty work so that their own tracks were covered. Many pirates were cruel, murderous and often crazy criminals fleeing from justice. Privateers, on the other hand, held official government contracts called letters of marque. They were hailed – at least in their own countries – as national heroes and builders of empires.

▲ **FISHERMAN HERO**

Jean Bart's success as a pirate raised him from his humble beginnings as a fisherman's son. He was born in Dunkirk on the north coast of France in 1651. At this time, many young men from the area were recruited by the local corsairs, privateers who attacked English shipping. Bart's daring exploits against the British and Dutch made him a hero in France.

▲ **THE WILD BUNCH**

The buccaneers of the Caribbean included ne'er-do-wells of many nationalities. Many were French refugees from the island of St Kitts, which was a constant battleground between English and French settlers. They escaped to Hispaniola and set up base on the island of Tortuga. The buccaneers took their name from the *boucans*, the open stoves they used for smoking meat after a hunting expedition. They lived a riotous life of fighting and drinking.

◄ **JOINING HARRY'S ARMY**

Henry Morgan surveys a line-up of potential recruits for his buccaneer army. Morgan joined a British expedition sent to capture Jamaica from the Spanish in 1654. His armies of buccaneers fought and raided throughout the Spanish Main. As a privateer, Morgan was praised by the authorities, knighted, and made Lieutenant-Governor of Jamaica. However, he led a wild life and drank himself to death in 1688, aged 53.

◢ A DIRE WARNING

The body of a pirate swinging from a gibbet is pointed out as a warning to a young man being taken to join his ship. In the 1700s, apprentices (young people learning a trade) who were unable or unwilling to work hard were often sent to sea. There they mixed with ships' crews that often included teenage rebels, jailbirds and ruffians. These were just the sort of people who were likely to become pirates if they were given the chance.

▲ MUTINY – AND THEN WHAT?

A British naval crew mutinies (refuses to obey orders) in 1797 as a protest against terrible conditions on board ship. As a result, they may well face hanging. The main alternative might be a life of piracy. It would be no worse than what they were used to.

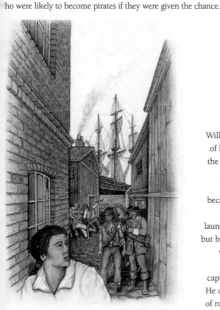

A NEW LIFE ▶

William Lewis tears out a lock of his hair and dedicates it to the Devil in the heat of battle. Lewis (c.1684–1718) was a prizefighter before he became a pirate captain. Such no-turning-back oaths launched many a pirate career, but brave talk was often all that was left to many desperate men. Lewis was finally captured in the Bahamas. He called for a drink of rum as he faced the gallows.

◢ RECRUITMENT TECHNIQUES

A young man is spotted by a pirate crew. After a knock on the head, he will probably wake up on a ship already out at sea. Naval, merchant and pirate ships all pressed (forced) crew into service.

Wild Women

In the high days of piracy, women were banned from sailing as members of the crew, often on pain of death. It was an old sailing tradition. Sea captains wanted their crew to sail the ship and fight rather than quarrel over women. However, throughout history some women have rebelled against their exclusion from the world of men. Women pirates wore trousers and shirts not only for disguise, but also because they were more practical for fighting and hauling ropes. They are, in any event, unlikely to have convinced other crew members that they were really men, for the ships in which they sailed offered little privacy.

In lawless, war-torn areas such as the Caribbean in the 1700s, a life of crime at sea offered the possibility of greater riches than the tough life on land. Mary Read and Anne Bonny persuaded a pirate captain to take them on and proved that women could be just as ruthless as the men.

◄ PIRATE PRINCESS

Princess Alwilda of Gotland in Sweden was the first woman pirate we know of. She and her all-female crew left a trail of destruction around the coast of the Baltic Sea around 1,500 years ago. Alwilda turned pirate to avoid marrying the prince of her father's choice. In this picture, she is shown, rather inappropriately, wearing a Victorian sailor suit.

Spanish doubloon such as these wer among the hoar captured by Lad Mary Killigrew

◄ WICKED LADY

On New Year's Day 1583 the Spanish ship *Maria* was driven by storms into Falmouth Bay, in Cornwall. It anchored below Arwennack House (*left*), home of the respectable Killigrew family. One dark night, Lady Mary Killigrew boarded the vessel with her servants and tied up the crew. She then slipped ashore, while her men sailed out of the harbour. They threw the Spaniards overboard, pocketed their gold and sailed to Ireland, where they sold the cargo at a handsome profit. Some accounts of the tale say that Lady Mary's husband, Sir John, was at that time a government official whose job was to combat piracy in Cornwall!

▲ THE LUCK OF THE IRISH

The maze of small islands in Clew Bay (on the Atlantic coast of Ireland) provided the perfect base for a fleet of pirate galleys in the 1560s. The ships were commanded by a noblewoman called Grainne Ni Mhaille or Grace O'Malley. Her Irish nickname was Mhaol, meaning bald or crop-headed. After years of looting, Grace managed to escape justice and in 1593 she sailed in person to negotiate a peace deal with the English queen Elizabeth I.

◄ BONNY AND BRAVE

In the 1700s, Irish-born Anne Bonny and her father sought a new life in North America. Anne eloped with a sailor to the Bahamas but soon left him for the dashing pirate Calico Jack Rackham (so called because of his calico cotton trousers). Witnesses giving evidence at the trial of Bonny and Read described the women as heavily armed and violent. They had fought their final battle more fearlessly than the men. Like her companion, Anne escaped the gallows because she was pregnant.

MARY READ ►

When she was a teenager in England, Mary Read joined the army disguised as a boy. She married a Flemish soldier, but after he died she headed for the Caribbean. The ship she sailed on was captured by pirates. Mary was clearly impressed by the incident, for she soon joined the crew of pirate captain Calico Jack Rackham. Her favourite crew member turned out to be another woman disguised as a man – Anne Bonny. Mary escaped the gallows because she was pregnant, but she died in prison of a fever before the baby was born

▲ THE CHINESE WIDOW

One of the most ruthless pirates of the South China Seas was a woman. Qing Er Sou, or Madam Cheng, was the widow of a pirate chief who had died in 1807. She took command of her husband's pirate fleet which had a total crew of 50,000. One way she kept control was by punishing such crimes as theft, by beheading. For three years, the fleet wreaked havoc, raiding ships and villages, and fighting rival pirates. In 1810, she successfully negotiated a pardon from the Chinese government.

The Captain's Finery

A pirate captain who had found wealth liked to show off with fine clothes like this jacket trimmed with gold braid. In the Bahamas in 1718, the pirate Denis McKarthy went to the gallows with blue ribbons at his neck, wrists, knees and cap and defiantly kicked off his silver-buckled shoes into the crowd. Viking chieftains wore beautifully worked metal helmets and faceguards, while their crews wore simple leather caps. The buccaneers of the 1630s wore filthy linen shirts with breeches and coarse hide boots. A hundred years later, sailors wore wide calico trousers, loose shirts and kerchiefs.

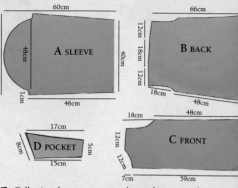

1 Following the measurements shown above, copy the patterns for the sleeves, front and back jacket, and pocket flaps on to t paper. Cut the pattern pieces out.

You will need: thin white paper or newspaper, measuring tape, pencil, scissors,1.5 x 1.5m red felt, pins, red thread, needle, iron, tailor's chalk, 5 brass buttons, 2m gold braid.

Captain William Kidd was a pirate with a respectable past and might have dressed as shown in the painting (left). Kidd had a place in fashionable New York society as a wealthy merchant. But he missed his early life as a privateer for the British Government and returned to sea in the 1690s. Bad luck and bad crews forced him to turn pirate.

3 Fold each sleeve lengthwise. Pin the open sides together about 1cm in, all the way from the cuff to the beginning of the curve of the armhole.

4 Sew a seam of running stitches along the pins. Make the second sleeve in the same way. Remove the pins and turn the sleeves right side out.

5 Lay the back flat. Put the two front jacket pieces or top, with sides lining up fron and back. Then pin and sew t pieces together at the shoulde

9 Turn the jacket right side out. Pin the pocket flaps upside down on the front, and sew into place. Iron the flaps forward over the sewing.

10 Using thread or tailor' chalk, mark where the buttons are to go. They should be at 6cm intervals, 1cm from the edge. Sew on the buttons.

Pin the back section **B** on to the felt and cut it out. Fold the rest of the felt in half and pin sections **A**, **C** and **D** on to double thickness to make two of each.

1 Take a square of fabric about 60 x 60cm. Fold it in half diagonally.

2 Place the triangle over your head. Long edge is at the front, the point at the back.

3 Take the front ends around your head. Tie them over the triangle point at the back.

4 Tuck the loose ends into the band formed around your head. They go near the knot.

6 Now pin the sides to the back, from the bottom to the beginning of the semicircular armhole. Sew the sections together and remove the pins.

7 Lay out the body of the jacket and carefully insert the sleeves into the armholes. The sleeves should lie inside the jacket.

8 Pin the top of the sleeve into the armhole. Make little pleats as you go so that it fits. Sew the sleeves into position and remove pins.

To finish, sew the remaining braid on to the pocket flaps. Pirate captains of the 1700s liked such finishing touches on their jackets. Pirates often wore their own versions of the fashions of the time. Their clothes were frequently stolen from their victims. You can wear your dashing pirate coat with a pair of baggy trousers, a sash around your waist, a neckerchief, a headscarf and a shirt.

11 Try the jacket on and turn up the sleeve cuffs the right length for your arm. ..n, then sew braid around the ..ff about 1cm from the top.

12 Cut the braid into five strips 14cm long. Fold the strips in half. Pin, then sew them on the front of the jacket to align with the buttons opposite.

Life at Sea

U ntil the 1800s no one gave much thought to conditions at sea for the common seaman, and life was hard for all sailors, pirates or not. Wooden ships of the 1600s and 1700s were cramped and uncomfortable. Pirate ships were often especially crowded because they had to take extra hands along to sail any captured vessels. The ships were unwieldy and pitched and tossed in the swell. Below deck, rats scampered in the darkness. The timbers creaked, and the bilges slopped in the depths of the ship. Lanterns shed a dim light, but open flames were forbidden, for fear that a spark would set off the gunpowder store. Bed was a lurching hammock or the corner of a storeroom. To go to the toilet, you had to squat over the head (a slatted box at the ship's bow with a hole open to the waves). Injury and disease were rife, and medical skills and supplies were minimal.

▲ GALLEY SLAVES

Corsair galley slaves are forced to row for their lives. They are whipped mercilessly and given barely enough food to stay alive. Along the Barbary Coast of Africa in the 1500s and 1600s, life was miserable whether you were a Christian slave on a Muslim corsair ship or a Muslim slave on a Christian corsair. In earlier times, oarsmen of the Greek pirate galleys also had a hard life, rowing on hard benches and exposed to the burning sun, but at least they were free.

PUTTING ASHORE ▶

A ship's company goes ashore on a coral island to re-stock. Storage casks were filled with fresh water, and on tropical islands, there were coconuts and fresh fruit to pick. The crew could fish, and hunt seabirds, wild animals and giant turtles for fresh meat. When Captain Kidd's crew landed on the Laccadives (modern Lakshadweep) off the coast of India in the late 1600s, they also plundered and terrorized local villages.

◀ BAD COMPANY

Pirates drank and gambled to break the boredom of a long voyage. Most were rough seamen, and many had long lived on the wrong side of the law. Fights were common. In 1697, the Scottish privateer Captain William Kidd killed one of his own crew, gunner William Moore, by smashing him over the head with a bucket. About 20 years later, Blackbeard shot his ship's master, Israel Hands, through the knee. Frayed tempers were a particular problem when a ship was becalmed for days through lack of wind.

◀ DISHING IT UP

The ship's cook creates another disgusting meal. On a long voyage, most food had to be preserved by salting and drying, although hens might be kept on board for fresh eggs and meat. Biscuits called hard tack were often riddled with weevils (insects). Chinese pirates are on record as eating the ship's rats. Lack of vitamin C from fresh fruit and vegetables in the diet led to a horrible disease called scurvy.

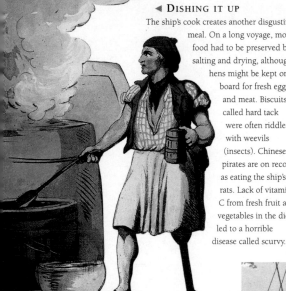

▲ SLUNG BETWEEN THE CANNON

A ship's crew starts a drinking bout on the gundeck. Heavy cannon were rolled back from the gunports and secured with ropes. Tables were slung from the beams, so that they could easily be stowed away during battle. Cloth hammocks, a South American invention, could also be cleared away quickly. They were used on British ships from 1597.

▲ SCRUBBING THE DECKS

A group of regular sailors is ordered to scrub the deck. Pirates were used to scenes like this on naval and merchant ships they had sailed on. The jobs still had to be done on pirate ships to keep the vessel seaworthy, but crews shared the work. They agreed a set of rules to cover aspects of everyday life such as care of fighting equipment and sharing of prizes from victims' ships. They could even elect to overthrow the captain.

▲ ALL IN A DAY'S WORK

Days at sea were an almost endless round of hard labour. Cannon were cleaned and kept in good running order. Heavy sails were raised and furled with changes in wind speed and direction, spars and masts repaired after battles or storms, frayed ropes spliced and joined. The pirates worked in watches (four-hour shifts), taking it in turns to sail the ship and to be on the lookout for land – and their next victim.

Drinking and Eating

Pirates drank water and ale from their tankards. Alcohol probably made the food go down more easily. You can tell how bad food on board ship must have been from the slang of the 1760s. Junk was the sailors' name for bits of old rope – and also their nickname for salted beef or pork, which tasted much the same. Dried peas and hard tack biscuits did little to improve the diet. Sometimes unfavourable winds forced a ship to be at sea so long that supplies ran out. This happened to the intrepid pirate Bartholomew Roberts and his crew in 1720, when they ran out of fresh water after 3,200km at sea. They drank seawater, which made them very sick.

You will need: 30 x 50cm thin card, ruler, pencil, scissors, masking tape, newspaper, 10 x 10cm thick card, cup of flour, about ½ cup of water, mixing bowl, spoon, fine sandpaper, silver paint, paintbrush, non toxic water-based varnish, bradawl or hole punch, large wire, paperclip, pliers.

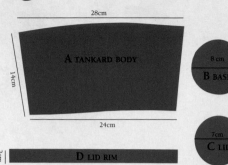

28cm

A TANKARD BODY

14cm

24cm

8 cm

B BASE

7cm

C LID

2cm

D LID RIM

25cm

1 Copy these tankard templates on to thin card using the measurements shown. Carefully cut out all of the pieces.

3 Twist some newspaper into a thin sausage. Use masking tape to stick it around the bottom of the cylinder. Make a thinner twist for the top rim.

4 To make the handle, make an even thinner twist of newspaper about 23cm long. Wrap masking tape tightly around it as you go.

5 Bend the newspaper twist into a handle shape. Tape the top end to the rim of the tankard. Tape the other end three-quarters of the way dow

Drinking sessions on shore were often wild and violent. The buccaneers of the Caribbean even mixed their rum with gunpowder. These cardboard figures show Blackbeard's crew feasting. They were designed for a toy theatre about 100 years after the death of the old villain. Blackbeard liked to issue challenges to other pirates. He once bet his crew that he could survive the longest in a small, closed hold filled with suffocating fumes. He won the bet!

9 Coat each strip of the newspaper with paste. Lay them, three layers thick, all over the tankard. Cover both the inside and outside surfaces.

10 Leave the tankard in a warm place to dry. W' hard, rub the surface smooth with sandpaper. Paint and the varnish when the paint is dry.

Bend section **A** into a cylinder to make the body of ~~the~~ tankard. Secure with masking ~~tape~~. Tape section **B** to the wider ~~end~~ of the cylinder.

HARD TACK

You will need:
450g wholemeal flour, ⅛ tsp salt, bowl, water, fork, rolling pin, greased baking tray, knife.

1 Put the flour and salt in a bowl. Add cold water, a spoonful at a time. When it binds together, knead it into a dough.

2 Leave for about 30 minutes. Roll the dough to about 1cm thick. Place on the baking tray. Score into biscuit shapes.

3 Bake in the oven (420°F/215°C/Gas Mark 7) for 30 minutes. Remove from oven and leave to cool and harden.

6 Curve the lid rim **D** around the lid section **C**. Tape to ~~se~~cure. Scrunch up some ~~ne~~wspaper into the shape shown ~~in~~ Step 7 and tape it on the lid.

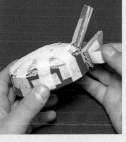

7 Draw a 4cm diameter circle on the thick card and cut out a quarter circle shape. Cut a 4 x 2cm strip of thick card. Tape the pieces to the lid as shown above.

8 Slowly add the water to the flour and mix to a smooth paste like pancake batter. Tear newspaper into lots of narrow strips.

The finished tankard has the authentic battered look of the pewter tankards that would have been used by pirates. Pewter is a hardwearing metal alloy, from which many frequently used objects were made. Your model is more decorative than functional. The non-toxic varnish makes your tankard waterproof, but because it is made of cardboard, it will be less hardwearing than a pewter one.

11 Pierce the centre of the quarter circle on the lid ~~wi~~th the bradawl. Straighten the ~~pa~~perclip and push it half way ~~th~~rough the hole.

12 Place the lid on the tankard. Use pliers to bend the two ends of the paperclip downwards and twist them together under the handle.

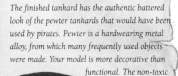

Finding the Way

Until about AD1000, sailors had no reliable instruments or maps to help them steer a course. They had to take their bearings from the sun and stars, watch the patterns of currents and waves, or follow coastlines where they could recognize landmarks. The Vikings only discovered Greenland and North America when they were blown westwards by storms. Asian pirates could judge their course by rain-bearing monsoon winds that blew in the same direction each year.

By the 1400s, seafarers could measure the positions of the sun and stars to help them establish their latitude using rod-like instruments called staffs. To find out the longitude position was only possible when the marine chronometer was invented in the early 1700s. This could keep accurate time despite temperature changes and movement at sea, so that sailors could estimate how far they had travelled from a fixed point in time. They calculated speed by trailing a log tied to a rope – from which the word log-book comes. This was a record of the distance covered and the compass directions followed.

▲ A SLIP AND YOU'RE DEAD!
A pirate shins up the slippery ropes to take his turn on lookout from the main top (also known as the crow's nest). He is over 30m above deck, and the ship is pitching on the waves. He makes sure he climbs on the windward side of the ship so that the wind presses him securely against the ratlines.

▲ LOOKING FOR LAND
A telescope like this 1700 example was a godsend to seafarers. It meant they could see land long before it was visible with the naked eye. Sailors also looked for birds and at waves and currents for clues which might indicate that they were near to land.

◀ MEDIEVAL MAPS
A monk of the 1300s measures distances with a pair of dividers. Maps, based on astronomical observations and travellers' reports of time and distance, varied in accuracy. They were copied by hand, kept in royal libraries and monasteries, and often considered too precious to be taken to sea.

COMPASS POINTS ▶
A pirate captain would have loved this 1568 gilded brass sundial compass – but to sell! He would have used more rough-and-ready instruments. Combined with a map, the magnetic compass made navigation less hit-and-miss, as it orientated itself north-south. However, versions that were reliable at sea were not available until the 1500s.

▲ TELESCOPIC VISION

A crew member on a British East Indiaman of the early 1800s peers through one of the gunports with his telescope. He may be sighting one of the French corsairs that plagued British merchant ships on their way back from the Far East. The telescope had improved considerably since it was first demonstrated by a Dutch spectacle-maker called Hans Lippershey in 1608. By the 1800s, it had become a precise and effective instrument for navigation and use in naval warfare.

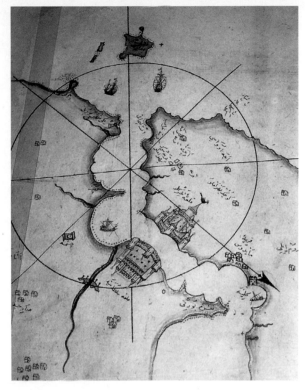

▲ BARBAROSSA'S ROADS

A fine 1525 map reveals routes taken by the Barbarossa brothers (Muslim corsairs who plundered Christian shipping). It covers the straits between the Mediterranean Sea and the Sea of Marmara. Good quality navigational maps like this were rare and highly valued if they were found on a captured ship. Coasts were painstakingly surveyed and charts drawn up by navigators who doubled as sea artists.

◀ SHIP TO SHORE

A crew member in the crow's nest works out the distance from ship to shore, and the firing range for the gunners. He uses a wooden cross staff to calculate the angle of the sun above the horizon and various other angles to make his calculations.

Charting the Waters

The area chosen for this map is the Spanish Main, which was a hotbed of pirates from the 1620s to the 1720s. When the Spanish first explored the Americas in the late 1400s, much of the world was unmapped territory. Naval expeditions were often sent to make detailed charts of distant waters for the use of trading ships. Most pirates had to make do with jotting down the details of islands, reefs, coastlines and river mouths as they sailed by, unless they happened to capture a ship with up-to-date charts. Books of detailed nautical charts, known as waggoners, were a valuable prize for any pirate captain. When sailing into an unknown harbour, ships had to take a local guide or pilot on board – at the point of a sword if necessary!

You will need: thick art paper approx 36 x 28cm, scissors, cold strong tea, paintbrush, pencil, black felt-tipped pen (fine), eraser, colouring pencils, ruler, 4cm diameter lid, 2cm diameter lid.

1 Cut out the paper to make a rectangle about 35 x 27cm. Make the edges wavy and uneven to give the map an authentic aged and worn appearance.

2 Scrunch up the paper tight into a bundle. Then open and smooth it out on a flat surface. Creases will remain, giving the map a used look.

4 Smooth out the paper. Stain the edges darker by brushing on more tea all the way around, from the outside inwards. Leave the paper to dry.

5 Copy the coastline from the finished map in Step 12 using your pencil. If you want, you can trace a map from another book and use that.

6 Draw over the coastline carefully with your black felt-tipped pen. Make sure you do not smudge the ink with your hand. Rub out the pencil lines.

You can try making a decorative map like this one of Puerto Rico. The Caribbean island was drawn by the French explorer Samuel de Champlain in 1599. The Spanish discovered Puerto Rico in 1493. It became known as the rich port, and was raided by the English seafarers Francis Drake and John Hawkins in 1595. In the 1700s the island was still described as a nest of pirates.

10 Draw around the 4cm lid to make a circle over your ship's position. Then draw an inner circle with the small lid to make the compass shape.

Paint cold, strong tea on to the paper. This stains it [do]wn to look like old, worn [par]chment. Then leave the paper [unt]il it is completely dry.

Look at all the co-ordinate lines on this Dutch map of 1650. They show where ships have plotted their position at sea. Many of the places on this map, such as Florida and Central America, were ruled by the Spanish at this time. The French, Dutch and British also wanted new land. If one of their privateers seized a Spanish ship, he would be delighted if there were maps of newly discovered countries on board.

7 Colour the land green, and the sea blue. Graduate the [col]ours, making them a little [da]rker along the coastline and [th]en fading inland or out to sea.

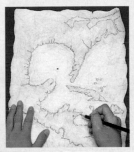

8 Choose three landmarks such as headlands. Use a pencil and ruler to draw lines from these to a spot in the sea to mark your ship's position.

9 Use the ruler and a black pencil to draw straight lines across this position, or co-ordinate, to look like the spokes of a wheel.

11 Draw small triangles pointing outwards from [th]e inner circle along the [co]-ordinate lines. Colour them in [a] bright colour.

12 You can add more decorative details such as arrow points on the compass, or dolphins in the sea and treasure chests on the land.

The best maps pirates could find would show safe ports and harbours, creeks and inlets. They also needed to know where there were dangerous coasts, currents and rocks. Maps had to be looked after well so that they did not wear out with heavy use and in the damp conditions at sea.

Flags of Terror

Viking raiding parties sometimes flew a flag that showed the sinister, all-seeing ravens of their chief god, Odin. Between AD1000 and 1500, ships flew royal flags or the colours of their home port, and later the national flags of their country. Some pirates flew national flags too, but mostly they despised them – except as a way of tricking the enemy. They preferred to fly flags that would create panic. Their message was that no quarter (no mercy) would be given and none would be expected in return. The Barbary corsairs and other early pirates often flew red flags. Some say that the term Jolly Roger is derived from the French description of these flags, *joli rouge* (pretty red). Others say that Old Roger was a nickname for the Devil.

By the 1700s, many pirate flags on European vessels were black, with the personal emblems of each pirate captain. In the South China Seas, each pirate squadron flew its own distinctively coloured flag.

▲ **A PIRATE GRAVE**
Many of the flags chosen by the pirate captains of the 1700s were inspired by popular engravings on tombstones. This one, in the Western Isles of Scotland, is thought to mark the grave of one of the pirates who plagued the coast in the 1600s and 1700s. The tombstones often featured skulls, bones and hourglasses. Graves like this can still be seen today.

▲ **PIRATES AHOY!**
Up goes the flag of Rhode Islander Thomas Tew, captain of the privateer turned pirate ship *Amity*. Pirates would often fly a false flag to the very last minute and then suddenly break out the Jolly Roger to confound and frighten their unprepared victims.

BLOOD-RED BANNER ▶
The flag flown by British pirate Christopher Moody (1694–1722) shows three symbols of piracy. The winged hourglass warns victims that the sands of time are running out for them. Arm-and-sword designs may have first been copied from the Barbary corsairs. The skull and crossbones suggest a fight to the death.

▲ **TRIPLE SKULL THREAT**
The long pennant (triangular flag) of Christopher Condent has room for three skulls. Condent was from Plymouth, England and captained the *Dragon* in the early 1700s. In 1719 he terrorized Red Sea shipping, seizing silks, spices and gold coins. Many of his crew were black West Africans escaping a life of slavery. Some eventually settled on the Indian Ocean island of Réunion, having done a deal with its French governor. Condent married a relative of the governor and retired to the French port of St Malo, in Brittany.

◀ DICING WITH DEATH

The first flag flown by Bartholomew Roberts shows the dashing pirate captain himself and a menacing skeleton clutching a spear. This was probably the flag Roberts flew on the *Royal Rover* as it sailed from Devil's Island (off South America) to Newfoundland in 1719–20. When the governors of two Caribbean islands, Martinique and Barbados, sent naval patrols after Roberts, he designed a flag showing their skulls crushed beneath his feet.

▲ RED BONES

The scarlet skeleton of Edward Low instilled fear in all those who saw it sailing off America's east coast in the 1720s. Low was an English merchant seaman turned pirate. He had a reputation for being a brutal man who enjoyed torturing his victims.

THE SIGN OF CALICO JACK ▶

Crossed cutlasses replaced bones on the flag of Calico Jack Rackham, who sailed with the women pirates Anne Bonny and Mary Read. Rackham was a cunning operator who escaped against the odds time after time.

In November 1720, his sloop was boarded by a British privateer commanded by Captain Jonathan Barnet. Rackham's boldness finally deserted him. He hid below decks and left the women to fight it out.

▲ DEATH'S HEAD

The basic skull and crossbones on a black background became the most familiar emblem of piracy. It was flown by the Irish captain Edward England who died on Madagascar in 1720. His ship, the *Fancy*, actually flew three flags – a skull and crossbones, a plain red flag and a red and white St George's cross, the national flag of England.

▲ LONG BEN'S BANNER

A simple death's head was flown by the Englishman known as the Arch-Pirate, Henry "Long Ben" Avery. When he was sailing master on a British privateer, Avery was elected captain when the crew mutinied. He was notorious for daring exploits on the Pirate Round such as attacking the Moghul emperor's flagship in 1695. Despite his fame and fortune, Avery died in poverty.

▲ FLYING THE JOLLY ROGER

A drawing in London's *Pall Mall* magazine of the 1800s shows a romantic idea of a pirate ship. The Jolly Roger flown from the stern is more likely to have been hoisted atop the main mast.

BLEEDING HEART ▶

The macabre flag of Edward Teach (Blackbeard) was feared throughout Virginia, the Carolinas and the West Indies. It flew on the *Queen Anne's Revenge*, which was patriotically named after the British queen and manned by a crew of 300.

Hoist the Jolly Roger

Pirates probably made flags at sea from scraps of cloth. They were handy at stitching as they had to mend sails. Some flags may have been made in piratical ports such as Nassau as well. Flags are raised on ropes called halyards and may be flown from any of a ship's masts. One carried on a staff at the prow of a ship is a jack, while a flag on the stern is an ensign. Flags indicate wind direction, identify the ship – often deceptively in the case of pirate vessels – and are used for signalling. If pirates deciphered signalling codes they could use them to confuse their victims.

1 Draw a skull and crossbones on the card as shown above. Place the card on a cutting board. Cut out the image. Do not lose the unattached eyes and nose!

2 Place the fabric flat on the newspaper. Centre the sten on the fabric, position the eyes and nose, and tape carefully in place. Sponge on the fabric pain

You will need: A2 sheet of stencil card or thin card, pencil, cutting board, craft knife, 23 x 68cm cleaned and ironed black cotton fabric, large sheet of newspaper, masking tape, white fabric paint, sponge, pins, black thread, needle, iron, 35cm thin rope (the flag rope), 3m thin rope (the pole rope), 2 toggles, 170cm length dowel, 3cm diameter, acrylic paint, stiff paintbrush, 2 screw-in metal eyes, 1cm diameter.

4 Take the 35cm piece of the thin rope (the flag rope). Tie a wooden toggle about 2cm from each end of the rope using a simple single knot.

5 Lay the flag face down. Then place the rope along the unsewn edge of the flag, about 2½cm from the edge. The toggles overlap each end.

6 Turn over the raw edge. Fo this edge over the rope and pin. Sew the rope to the top and bottom openings. Sew along the long fold to enclose the rope.

The flag of death flaps in a stiff breeze as Major Stede Bonnet rests on his musket. Bonnet was an unlikely pirate. He was a respected gentleman plantation owner in Barbados. Bored with life, he took up a life of piracy, as captain of a sloop. In 1717 he fell in with the rough Edward Teach (Blackbeard), who scorned Bonnet as a landlubber and tricked him out of his ship.

9 Place the crossing loops over one of the toggles on the flag. Pull both ends to tighten. Take one end of rope to the other toggle and tie with another clove hitch.

10 Paint the dowel flagpole When dry, screw one metal eye 25cm from one end. Screw the other eye on the same side, about 4cm from the top.

When the paint is dry, remove the stencil. Turn the ... face down and double-fold ... edge apart from the right ... one. Pin, sew, and iron flat.

DRAW A SKULL AND CROSSBONES

1 Use a pencil to draw a simple oval for the skull. Draw a diagonal cross centred beneath it.

2 Use the cross as a guide to add thickness to the bones. Draw in the knuckles at each end.

3 Separate the oval into two parts. Copy the outline of the jaw and the bottom edge of the skull.

4 Draw in two circles for the eye cavities. Add a small shape for the nose, and then draw in the teeth.

7 Make a clove hitch in the 3m pole. With one hand, turn the ... back to make a loop. With ... other hand, turn it forward to ... ke another loop.

8 Hold a loop in each hand. Put the right loop in front of the left one. Then take hold of the two loops firmly where they cross over each other.

You can stick your flag pole in a bucket of sand, or in your garden as a warning to intruders! Pull the rope gently through the metal eyes to hoist or lower the flag. If you had been living in the pirate haven of New Providence in the Bahamas, you could have earned some extra pocket money from your flagmaking. A sailmaker's widow who lived there used to make pirate flags in return for a bottle of brandy.

11 Thread the pole rope through the top metal ... e and along the pole. Take it ... rough the bottom eye, and ... ck to the middle of the pole.

12 Tie the two ends of the rope together with a reef knot (as shown on the pages Learning the Ropes) and pull firmly to tighten.

Pirate Ships

Throughout history, pirate ships have been much the same as other ships. They ranged from the oared galleys of ancient Greece and Rome to Viking longships, from the piraguas (little more than canoes with sails) of the early buccaneers to the neat sloops that sailed out of Nassau in the West Indies in the 1700s. In Asian waters there were Arab dhows, Chinese junks and Malayan galleys called prahus.

Many pirate ships were prizes – ships that had been stolen or captured. Pirates sometimes adapted these for their own use, for example by raising the bulwarks (upper sides) of a merchant vessel for extra protection against attack or by fitting new guns. The ships needed constant maintenance and were regularly beached for careening (cleaning and repairs). The hull was scraped clear of seaweed and barnacles. Timbers were caulked (sealed) with oakum (rope fibre) and pitch, and wood destroyed by burrowing marine worms was replaced.

▲ SPEED VERSUS SIZE
A small Dutch ship (*right*) nips around the Spanish treasure ship it is attacking. The Dutch started to send privateers after Spanish ships in the 1600s. They soon moved on from European waters to test their strength in the Caribbean.

◄ OAR POWER
Long, narrow Barbary corsairs of the 1500s to 1800s could turn and change speed quickly. They were rowed by up to 90 slaves, four or six to each oar. Sails were hoisted for extra power in a strong wind. The corsairs carried a formidable fighting force and were geared to short outings rather than ocean-going trips.

RACING SCHOONERS ▶
Small, fast and ocean-going schooners were being captured and used by pirates from the early 1700s. They were especially sought after by American privateers who attacked British merchant ships towards the end of the 1700s. Schooners are sleek and narrow, usually with two masts, two big sails and two foresails. A top square sail on the main mast was hoisted to give an extra boost to speed in a following wind.

Greek pirate galley, 500BC   Viking longship, AD900   Arab dhow, AD900   English galleon, 1500

◀ FRIGATE CHASE

The year is 1790 and a British naval frigate runs in a pirate ship called the *Liguria*. They exchange heavy fire, and the painting shows very clearly the damage caused to the sails by shot during the battle. Frigates were fast naval boats that served as small warships with around 20 guns. Pirates usually avoided frigates. Most of their vessels were captured merchant ships, and pirate crews were notoriously disorganized. They were rarely a match for heavily armed, well trained naval patrols.

SPEED WINS THE DAY ▲

A nifty pirate vessel buzzes around a floundering East Indiaman merchant ship like an angry wasp. The big British and Dutch Indiamen carried rich cargoes of porcelain, tea, silks and spices from the Far East. They were targeted by Maratha pirates along the western coast of India between 1690 and 1756. In the 1790s and 1800s, they were tailed and attacked by French privateers.

ORIENTAL SAILING ▶

Junks (the traditional wooden sailing ships of China) were still used by pirates in the 1920s. They have squared-off bows and a high stern and vary greatly in size. Junks were mostly used for trading, but they were often captured by pirates and fitted with guns. However, they were no match for the European warships that pursued them. Their sails, made of matting or coarse linen reinforced with bamboo, easily caught fire during battle.

Maltese corsair, 1660

East Indiaman, 1700

Pirate sloop, 1780

Brigantine, 1800

Learning the Ropes

Here are just three of the many knots that seamen had to learn to use on board. Galleys and sailing ships were creaking worlds of rope, wood and canvas. Knots were used to join or attach one thing to another (such as the ship to a mooring), to make loops or to shorten a rope. Ropes were needed when sails were furled (folded and secured) before a storm or unfurled to gain speed. Ropes were usually made from flax or hemp fibres. When they were not in use, they were coiled neatly. Sailors were expert at joining them by splicing and at mending frayed ends or making eye-holes. Sometimes they unpicked ropes with a marlinspike (a metal point that served as a weapon in many brawls).

You will need: two pieces of rope, about 1cm diameter, and 0.5–1m long. You may find it easier to have one piece of rope in a different colour when you are practising the sheetbend.

A simple, sturdy knot called the fisherman's bend is used to tie on the heavy rope needed to carry this anchor's weight. This iron ship's anchor dates from 1768. In ancient times, pirates used baskets of stone or lead as anchors.

THE BOWLINE

1 Hold a piece of rope near the top in one hand. With the other hand, twist the short end down and up so that the short end is looped over the long end.

2 Turn the loop towards you Hold the point where the rope crosses with one hand. W the other take the short end down through the loophole.

THE REEF KNOT

 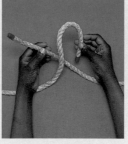 

1 Take two lengths of rope. Hold a piece in each hand. Pass the one on the left over the one on the right so that the two ropes cross over each other.

2 Hold the rope that is now on the right (or hold the point where the ropes cross) With the other hand, bring this rope around the back of the other.

3 Bring the same piece of rop forward and up over the other piece. Bring both right an left ends level, making a figure eight in between them.

THE SHEETBEND

1 Take two pieces of rope. Fold the end of the coloured rope back on itself to form a loop. Hold the neck of the loop firmly with your finger and thumb.

2 Keep holding the loop firmly in one hand. With your other hand, bring the white piece of rope behind and up through the loop.

3 Still holding the neck of th loop firmly, take the white rope up through the loop. Then take it behind the neck of the loop and forward.

3 Hold where the short end comes through the bottom the loop. Turn the loop bright. Bring the short end out d behind the long end of rope.

4 Bring the short end forward, making another loop at the bottom. You should now see three loops. Take the short end down through the middle loop.

5 Bring the short end down to lie beside the long end. Hold these two ends with one hand. Hold the top of the loop with the other and pull firmly.

The bowline is used to make a loop in the end of a rope. If it is tied correctly, the loop will not slip, although the knot is easy to untie. It is a useful knot for tying a boat to a mooring post.

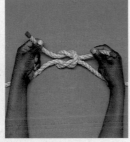

4 Cross the righthand end of the rope over and under the fthand end. Bring the end at is underneath up through the middle.

5 Pull both right and left ends at the same time to tighten the knot. You should be able to push the interlinking loops together and apart quite easily.

The reef knot comes undone quite easily, so a sailor would not use it on any rope that would have to bear weight. Its main use on board a sailing ship is to secure the reefing lines on the sails. These are pulled to gather in the sail to reduce its area in a strong wind.

4 Bring the white piece of rope around and over the utside of the loop. Then hread it through to cross back nder itself.

5 Let go of this end. Hold the long end of the white rope with one hand. Hold the neck of the loop with the other. Pull both to secure the knot.

The sheetbend is a strong and reliable knot for joining two pieces of rope together. It even works well if the ropes are of different thicknesses. The knots on these pages are still used by sailors today.

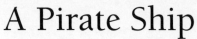

A Pirate Ship

A ship like the one in this picture outpaced and outmanoeuvred the heavier warships of its day. It is very like the *Adventure Galley,* which was built in 1695 for Scottish-born Captain William Kidd, a privateer and businessman who lived in New York City. Kidd's official mission was to hunt other pirates, but he ended up being accused of piracy himself. The *Adventure Galley* weighed 281 tonnes and was 38m long – bigger than many pirate vessels of the time. It was built in Deptford near London, England, and sailed to New York in April 1696 with a crew of 70. The following September, it left with a crew of 152, bound for the Indian Ocean. Under full sail, Kidd's ship could reach speeds of up to 14 knots (27km/hour). When the wind failed, it could be operated by the long oars, called sweeps. Although the ship was new, it leaked badly and was abandoned by Kidd in Madagascar, where it was stripped of valuables and burnt.

KEY		
1 *bowsprit*	11 *fore staysail*	22 *gundeck*
2 *mainsail*	12 *stern lantern*	23 *sweeps*
3 *spritsail*	13 *mizzen*	24 *bilges*
4 *topgallants*	14 *foremast*	25 *pumps*
5 *mizzen mast*	15 *gunwale*	26 *water casks*
6 *ratlines*	16 *foresail*	27 *gunport*
7 *yards*	17 *sail locker*	28 *anchor*
8 *jib*	18 *topsails*	
9 *foc's'le*	19 *magazine*	
10 *quarterdeck*	20 *crow's nest*	
	21 *shot locker*	

▲ COOK'S AREA

A kitchen on board ship is called a galley – a word that is also used for a large ship with oars. This one was in the fo'c's'le (the raised deck at the front of the ship). A bucket of sand stood by the stove to put out fires. Pirates often died from scurvy and cholera because of the poor diet.

◄ THE GUNDECK

Each of the *Adventure Galley's* 34 guns fired cannonballs that weighed 5.4kg each. This made it capable of taking on most merchant ships of the day. The ship carried 1,000 spare cannonballs in a locker in the hold and plenty of gunpowder in the magazine.

▲ THE CAPTAIN'S CABIN

The most comfortable part of the ship was the grand cabin at the stern. This was where the captain plotted the course of his voyage, gave orders to the crew and ate his meals. Here were his navigating instruments and his personal weapons, ready to hand in case of mutiny or sudden attack.

▲ THE CAPSTAN

The anchor was so heavy that it needed to be raised by a winding gear called a capstan. Bars were slotted into the top, so that it could be pushed round and round. It was backbreaking work, often done to the accompaniment of singing or fiddle music.

A Speedy Sloop

The word sloop was first used in 1629 to describe a small and nippy sailing ship suited to sailing coastal waters rather than great oceans. A typical sloop of those days had a long, standing bowsprit to support the small foresails. These small sails made the ship more manoeuvrable. A sloop usually had one mast, which carried the mainsail. The boats were used by Caribbean pirates because their shallow draught (depth under water) made them easy to beach in hidden creeks and lagoons. The pirate haunts of Bermuda and Jamaica became famous for building fine sloops in the 1700s.

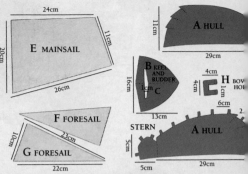

1 Copy templates A, B, C and H on to dark brown card, and D on light card. Copy the sail templates E, F, and G on to the fabric. F the mark for the mast hole on the deck section D with the knitting

You will need: one A2 sheet of dark brown card, one A3 sheet of light brown card, 40cm² cream cotton fabric, pencil, ruler, knitting needle, scissors, strong paper glue, adhesive tape, acrylic paints, paintbrush, cold stewed tea, 1.5m balsa wood dowel, 2.4cm diameter, cut into five pieces 12cm, 22cm, 13cm, 24cm and 50cm long, strong black sewing thread, strong darning needle.

5 Glue one side of the keel and rudder section C, leaving the edges unglued. Fold the section in half and pinch the glued areas so that they stick together.

6 Now put glue on the unglued edges. These stick on either side of the hull when you fit the keel and rudder section C into position.

7 Bend the tabs on the deck section D downwards. Put glue on the outside of each tab Ease the deck section D into th top of the boat's hull.

10 Oversew the top of the mainsail E to the 12cm dowel and the bottom to the 22cm dowel. Sew around the dowel and through the sail.

11 Glue the 13cm dowel about 6cm from the top of the 50cm dowel (mast) to make a long cross shape. This cross spar supports the tops of the sails.

12 Push the needle through the tops of the foresails E and G and the spar, then knot the thread. Join the bottom, pointed corners to the 24cm dowel.

13 Use the knitting needle to make an indent on t other side of the mast about 14cm up. Fill with glue. Insert the 22cm mainsail dowel.

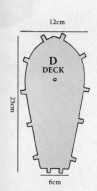

12cm

D DECK

25cm

6cm

...ut out all templates apart from ...e sails (**E, F and G**).

2 Cut 2½cm slits at the three points marked with a dotted line on hull section **A**. Overlap these to make the hull's curved shape. Glue them into position.

3 Cut three slits in exactly the same way on the second hull section **B**. This time, overlap them in the opposite direction. Glue the overlapping pieces into place.

4 Join the two hull sections **A** and **B** together on the inside with adhesive tape. Fold over the stern section to fit into the hull. Glue the tabs inside the hull.

...8 Paint thin brown lines along ...the length of the deck for ...anks. Paint a pale stripe along ...e top of the hull with gun ...oles and portholes.

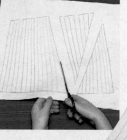

9 Draw vertical lines on to the sails. Cut out the sails with scissors. If you like, you can stain them by brushing with stewed tea.

...4 When the glue is dry, attach the mainsail **E** ...p. Take the thread around the ...wel at the top of the sail. Push ...through the spar and knot.

15 Glue the foot of the mast into the masthole. Glue bowsprit holder **H** in front of the mast. Fit the dowel holding the foresails into it.

Real sloops were built for trading, privateering and also for naval anti-piracy patrols. Your boat is neither seaworthy nor waterproof, so do not try sailing it in the bath.

Attack at Sea

In port, pirate spies would try to find out which ships had the richest cargoes, and when and where they were sailing. Pirates might trail their prey for days, keeping just out of sight – for the key to any successful attack was surprise. They might pose as a harmless merchant vessel, or lurk behind a headland and then suddenly sail out to confront their victims. Sometimes the most successful pirate actions were so foolhardy, that the enemy was simply dumbfounded. In the 1700s, the flamboyant pirate captain Bartholomew Roberts would cause panic by sailing into the thick of an enemy fleet, even though he was hopelessly outnumbered, but with drums beating and all guns blazing.

As soon as the target ship came within range – of catapults or bows and arrows in ancient times, or cannon from the 1400s onwards – serious shooting would begin. When the victim's ship was disabled, the pirates would prepare to board. The fate of the ship was then decided by hand-to-hand combat.

▲ BOARDING PARTY
The towering stern of a Spanish treasure ship looms above an attacking pirate crew. Their small boarding vessel is out of the galleon's firing line and so easy to control that the pirates can quickly come up alongside, ready to board.

▲ HOLDING FAST!
A pirate of the 1700s hurls a grappling iron over to the enemy ship. The iron's anchor-like hooks would take hold in the shrouds (ropes), so that the ship could be hauled close to. Pirates terrified their victims before boarding by cursing and yelling bloodthirsty threats. Fear was probably their most effective weapon.

◀ BATTERING RAMS
Pointed, metal-plated rams were fitted on the prows of ancient Greek and Roman galleys. They were designed to smash through the hull of an enemy ship. The galley would be rowed at maximum speed (perhaps 15km/hour) straight towards the enemy. Sailors from the Greek island of Rhodes devised some very crafty tricks. They used their oars to make the prow dip just before the point of collision, so that the ram holed the enemy ship as deeply as possible below the waterline.

◀ FINAL STAGE
A Turkish crew battles with Greek corsairs during the 1800s. Once two ships had closed with each other, a sea attack became more like a traditional land battle, with the ships serving as floating platforms for hand-to-hand combat. Turkish fleets often carried units of crack troops called janissaries.

Barbary galleys go into action against Venetian ships off the port of Patras in Greece, in 1751. From the Middle Ages onwards, Venice was one of the richest trading ports in Italy. Its shipping was regularly attacked by Uskok pirates (from what is now Croatia) and by Barbary corsairs from North Africa. Barbary galleys rarely travelled far from their home ports. They were designed for attack in the relatively calm Mediterranean rather than for the open ocean.

▲ PIRATES IN BONNETS

Pirates prepare to board an American vessel, going to great lengths to deceive their victims as to their true identity. Some of them crouch out of sight, armed to the teeth. Others are disguised as female passengers parading for the benefit of the American captain's telescope. Surprise is an essential weapon for a successful attack.

CHINESE TACTICS ▶

Chinese pirates board a ship from a simple rowing boat lowered from their main junk. Some of these small boats were armed with light guns and could carry up to 20 heavily armed pirates. Such attacks were still common in the South China Sea in the early 1900s. They became less effective when Dutch and English steam-powered gunboats were introduced to the area.

Fancy Figurehead

Decorative prows and figureheads have been put on ships since ancient times. Many were designed to bring good luck to the ship or to keep evil at bay. The prows of the galleys used by pirates and pirate hunters in ancient Rome often rose into a great curve that was ornately carved and painted or gilded. Some ancient Mediterranean galleys were decorated with big eyes (to ward off evil), victory wreaths, animals or figures. The prows of Viking longships were often carved into snarling dragon heads, which must have looked terrifying as a raiding party emerged from a ghostly sea mist.

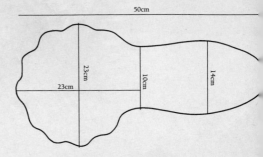

1 Following the measurements shown above, copy the basic figurehead shape on to the large piece of corrugated cardboard.

You will need: *60 x 30cm corrugated cardboard, pencil, ruler, scissors, a lot of old newspapers, masking tape, cup of flour, about ½ cup of water, bowl, fork, fine sandpaper, red, white and black acrylic paints, thick paintbrush, white card, craft knife, glue, thin paintbrush.*

Ajax, legendary hero of the Trojan Wars in ancient Greece, is the model for this splendid figurehead. He stood at the head of a 74-gun ship of the 1800s. Most naval patrol ships and some of the larger vessels captured as pirates' prizes had splendid figureheads. However, smaller, workaday pirate vessels were rarely so fancy.

4 Cover the whole base with a layer of paper balls. Add extra layers to the chest and face. Add an extra, fist-sized piece for the nose. Leave space for the eyes.

5 Twist the newspaper into sausages for jaw, lips and brows. Make two thick pieces fo the paws (see Step 10 for shape Tape everything into place.

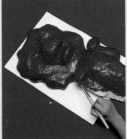

8 Make two table tennis ball-sized eyes from paste and newspaper. Leave everything in a warm place until dry and hard. Smooth with sandpaper.

9 Use the thick brush to paint the front and back of the figurehead in a bright colour. This figure is red, but rich yellow or blue would be good too.

10 Cut white card triangle for claws and teeth. Make slits in the paws and mouth with a craft knife, then glue teeth and claws into them.

Carefully cut out all round the figurehead shape. It will easier if you do a section at a time, as shown above, and you will not bend the board.

3 Scrunch up sheets of newspaper into tight balls. Place each ball on top of the cardboard cutout. Tape them on with the masking tape.

Here is an official lion figurehead like your model. Lions were standard designs for small British fighting ships from the early 1600s to the early 1800s. Individual figurehead designs were usually found only on large, important warships. This lion, which dates from around 1715, was probably on a sloop.

5 Put the flour into the bowl, and, mixing all the time with fork, gradually add water. The paste should be thick and smooth like pancake batter.

7 Tear lots of newspaper into strips. Dip these into the paste and cover the front and back of the figure with three layers of strips.

▲ Prows on the galleys of ancient Greece and Rome were not merely decorative. They doubled as vicious rams, which could slice into the hull of an enemy ship.

11 Paint the eyeballs white. When the paint is dry, add a black dot for the pupils. Glue the eyeballs on. Paint on the eyebrows and nostrils.

12 Use the fine paintbrush and the black paint to paint in other decorative details such as the fur.

Real figureheads were carved from wood and then painted. They were then mounted above the ship's cutwater (the part of the prow that slices through the waves).

Coastal Raids

Ships were never the only target for pirates. They raided coastal settlements in search of treasure, food or villagers they could sell as slaves. The Vikings were even prepared to join forces with rival crews, sail up rivers far inland, and attack whole cities. They besieged Paris in AD885 and pulled down London Bridge in 1009.

In 1627 the inhabitants of Reykjavik in Iceland were astounded to be raided, plundered and enslaved by Barbary corsairs from North Africa. This fleet was led by Dutchman Jan Jansz, who called himself Murad Rais. He was one of many European seafarers who turned Turk (joined the other side) and fought for the Muslim Barbary corsairs. It was these renegades who, for a time, persuaded the North Africans to break with custom and sail further afield.

Pirate trickery worked just as well on land as at sea. In 1719 the Welsh pirate Howell Davis managed to convince the commander of a Royal Africa Company fort in Gambia that he was a legitimate trader from Liverpool. Davis overpowered his host during dinner, and sailed off with gold bars and ivory from the company store.

▲ **MARCH OF DEATH**
A bloodthirsty crew of Vikings is carved on a gravestone. The warriors are armed with swords and battle axes. The carving may record the events of June AD793, when Viking pirates descended on the little island of Lindisfarne, off the north-east coast of England. They plundered the monastery, murdered the monks and then set fire to the buildings.

▲ **LAND HUNGRY**
Viking pirates from Scandinavia scan the coastline, searching out weak points in the defences. They will run their longships ashore, and attack with axes, spears, swords and burning arrows. Green hills were particularly appealing to Vikings in search of good land where they could settle. Much of their homeland in Scandinavia was poor heathland, barren mountain or snowy forest.

◄ **CATTLE RAIDERS**
A buccaneer rounds up stolen cattle during a raid on Santo Domingo on the island of Hispaniola. Raiders would sell cattle meat and hides to passing ships and make a useful profit. The cattle owners often suffered more than the loss of their animals. Many were tortured and killed by the buccaneers. Today, Hispaniola is occupied by the Dominican Republic and Haiti. During the 1500s and most of the 1600s, it was all ruled by Spain and under constant attack. From the 1630s, the west of the island became a base for the buccaneers.

◄ SPANISH-HELD TREASURE

An evil-looking bunch of buccaneers sacks the port of Cartagena, the largest Spanish city on the Caribbean coast of South America. In the 1630s, a steady stream of mule trains carried silver from the mines of Peru to be shipped back to Spain. Some Spanish towns were held to ransom by privateers and buccaneers time and time again.

▲ BUCCANEER ARMY RAID

In 1668, Henry Morgan led an army of English and French buccaneers into the Cuban town of Puerto del Principe (modern Camaguey). Over 700 heavily armed buccaneers marched inland, fighting their way mercilessly into the Spanish-ruled town. They killed a hunded soldiers and took many hostages. Local people were locked in churches while the buccaneers stole valuables from their homes. This was the first of Morgan's brutal, but very effective raids.

◄ HUMAN CARGO

A pirate crew seizes slaves from West Africa. Throughout history, slave trading and piracy went hand in hand. In the 1600s and 1700s, pirates could make a very large profit selling slaves to the new colonies in the Americas, at 10 to 15 times what they had paid for them. The pirates bartered with tribal chiefs, exchanging cheap gifts or currency for the slaves. Sometimes they kidnapped the slaves themselves.

Hand Weapons

A ccording to the ship's rules drawn up by pirate Captain George Lowther in the 1720s, the first crew member to spot a sail on the horizon would be rewarded with the best pistol on that ship, if it was captured. Personal weapons were the tools of a pirate's trade, and captured weapons were highly valued prizes. Pirates cared for their arms, cleaning them regularly and keeping them dry, for their lives depended on the weapons being in good working order.

Over the ages, a pirate's personal arms included every type of weapon imaginable – clubs, spears, daggers, swords, pistols and muskets. Some weapons became particularly associated with pirates. The Vikings are remembered for their battle axes. The swords of the Barbary corsairs were of the highest quality steel and finely crafted. The buccaneers of the Caribbean were famed as sharpshooters (experts with the musket and the flintlock pistol). Pirates of south-east Asia used spears, darts from blowpipes and very ornate swords – some of the handles were decorated with human hair. The most common and useful pirate weapon was probably the cutlass, a sword used by pirates and other sailors from the 1600s onwards.

◀ BUTCHER'S KNIFE
The simple but deadly cutlass may have its origins in the long knives used by the first buccaneers to butcher their cattle. A guard protects the hand and the blade is short and broad compared with a sword. Cutlasses, pikes and axes were used by the ship's company, while a pirate captain or naval officers might carry more elaborate swords.

▲ STRAIGHT TO THE POINT
A bold thrust of the cutlass at the throat of a senior officer, and the battle is as good as won. The sturdy cutlass was the standard weapon for close fighting until the late 1800s. It was less likely than a rapier to be caught in the ropes and sails on board ship.

◀ MAD MUSKETEERS
Wielding a musket was not easy, especially on an unsteady deck. A long rod was needed to reload, and the muzzle rested on a special support (the musket rest) ready for firing. Nevertheless, rust-proof muskets decorated with brass were specially designed for use at sea in the late 1600s. The weapons were also used by buccaneer armies of the 1600s when they raided the cities of the Spanish Main. Effective firing range was about 100m. A spark from a flint ignited the gunpowder charge and fired the lead musket ball.

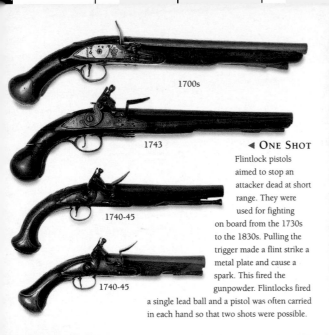

1700s

1743

1740-45

1740-45

◀ ONE SHOT
Flintlock pistols aimed to stop an attacker dead at short range. They were used for fighting on board from the 1730s to the 1830s. Pulling the trigger made a flint strike a metal plate and cause a spark. This fired the gunpowder. Flintlocks fired a single lead ball and a pistol was often carried in each hand so that two shots were possible.

▲ CHINESE DAGGERS
European passengers panic as Chinese pirates board a French steamship in the 1900s. Chinese pirates fought with firearms, bamboo spears, lethal-edged pikes and short swords with hooked blades. Victims were often beheaded. Piracy continued in the South China Sea until the 1920s.

◀ FIGHTING AT CLOSE QUARTERS
A naval crew boards a Barbary corsair, with cutlasses drawn. At close quarters, these short slashing swords were much more effective than long stabbing swords, such as rapiers. One sailor uses his pistol butt as a club. This particular battle was in 1816 when a combined British and Dutch naval fleet attacked the North African port of Algiers.

Cut-throat Cutlass

The swords carried by pirates varied greatly over the ages. Ancient Greek pirates might fight with a leaf-shaped blade about 60cm long or with a curved cut-and-thrust blade called a *kopis*. Their Roman enemies fought with a short sword called the *gladius*. Viking swords were long and double-edged, for heavy slashing. The rapier, introduced in the 1500s, was a very light sword with a deadly, pointed blade, but was too long and delicate for close-range fighting on board ship. The cutlass was the ideal weapon for that. The best quality steel was made by the Arabs, and would have used by Barbary corsairs.

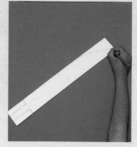

1 Lay one piece of the stiff card on a flat surface. Use a pencil to outline carefully the shape of the cutlass blade and hilt on to the cardboard.

2 Cut out the shape and use this as a template to lay on the second piece of card. Draw around the template and then c out a second cutlass shape.

You will need: *2 pieces of stiff card 45 x 5cm, pencil, scissors, glue, newspaper, masking tape, 1 piece stiff card 30 x 10cm, 1 cup of flour, about ½ cup of water, mixing bowl, fork, fine sandpaper, brown and silver acrylic paint, two 2.5cm paintbrushes, black felt-tipped pen, ruler, wood varnish.*

5 Take the third piece of card measuring 30 x 10cm. Draw the cutlass handle shape to fill the whole length of the card. Carefully cut it out.

6 Hold the narrow stem of the handle in one hand and scissors in the other. Cut down the middle of the wide end to about 2.5cm short of the stem.

7 Tape the narrow stem of the handle to the end of the cutlass hilt. Bend the rest of the handle round to slot over the curved edge of the blade.

The characters of Blackbeard the Pirate and Abdulla the Prince fight with cutlasses in this toy theatre production of the 1800s. The excitement and drama of a sword fight became a popular feature of many swashbuckling plays, pantomimes and, later, films about pirates.

12 Paint the cutlass blade and handle with two coats of acrylic paint. Allow each coat of paint to dry thoroughly before you apply the next.

3 Lay the two matching sections on top of each other. Glue them together. The double thickness gives the finished cutlass extra strength.

4 Twist newspaper into thick strips to wind around the hilt. This should be enough to make a thick handgrip. Bind the newspaper with masking tape.

Cutlasses were still being used 200 years after they were first introduced. In this vicious clash of 1809, Lieutenant John Turner and his British crew were overwhelmed by a Chinese pirate crew. The rivers and islands around the major international port of Canton (Guangzhou) were thick with pirates. The Europeans called them Ladrones, from the Portuguese word for robbers.

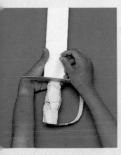

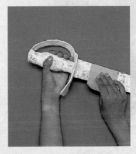

8 Make sure the oval lies flat against the hilt (to form a hand guard). Use masking tape to seal the slit and to secure the handle to the blade.

9 Put the flour in a bowl and slowly add water, a spoon at a time, mixing as you go. The paste should be smooth and thick like pancake batter.

10 Tear newspaper into short strips, coat these with paste and cover the whole of the cutlass three layers thick.

11 Leave the cutlass in a warm place for several hours. When completely hard and dry, smooth with sandpaper.

13 Leave the background paint surface to dry completely. Then use the black pen and a ruler to draw details on the blade, as shown above.

14 Finally, use a clean brush to apply a coat of wood varnish. This will toughen the cutlass as well as giving it a menacing glint.

The true cutlasses used by pirates and sailors from the 1600s onwards would have had a steel blade and a brass or iron hilt (handle). To stop the blade rusting – a problem you will not have with yours – the pirates would have rubbed grease on the blade.

Fire and Smoke

The aim of a pirate attack was to disable a ship, not to destroy it, and so make sure there was something left to steal. In ancient times, this was often achieved by firing flaming arrows into the rigging of enemy ships.

Gunpowder (a mixture of saltpetre, sulphur and charcoal) was invented in China in the AD800s. The Arabs knew of gunpowder by the 1200s and called it Chinese snow. However, it could not be effectively used as ammunition until bronze or iron barrels strong enough to contain the explosive force were made in the 1300s. Cannon became a standard fitting on fighting ships from the early 1500s, but accidents were common. Gunpowder was dangerous stuff, especially when handled by drunken or careless crews. Some buccaneers even tried mixing it with their rum and drinking it! In 1669 the magazine (the place where the gunpowder was stored) blew up on the Welsh pirate Henry Morgan's ship, the *Oxford*. Over 200 buccaneers were killed.

Pirates of the 1700s were expert at making hand grenades (wooden or iron pots filled with explosives). They also packed boats with gunpowder, set a fuse and let them drift into the enemy fleet. These boats were known as *brûlots* (fireships).

▲ Greek Fire

The notorious pirate fleets of the Mediterranean had access to a fearful new weapon between AD671 and 900. It was called Greek fire, an explosive cocktail of sulphur, quicklime and an inflammable spirit like petroleum, called naphtha. Jets of burning liquid were sprayed over the enemy from flamethrowers mounted on board ship and caused the most terrible injuries. Despite its name, Greek fire was probably first used in Byzantium (modern Istanbul).

▲ Round Shot

Cannon and musket balls like these were solid lumps of iron hurled at deadly speed from the muzzle of the gun. The ammunition expelled from a cannon or a musket by an explosion of gunpowder was called shot. Sometimes a lethal mixture of small iron pieces called grapeshot was fired from cannon too.

End of an Era ▶

The Dutch and English join forces in a fiery end to the centuries-long reign of the Barbary pirates. Following this dramatic 1816 sea battle off the corsair stronghold of Algiers, more than 1,000 Christian slaves were freed. It was announced that piracy was at an end, and many corsair galleys were scrapped or burned.

▲ LAND ATTACK

Fire from cannon and muskets blasts the field of battle as the Dutch under Pieter van der Deks plunder the Canary Islands in 1599. Ships' crews carrying out raids on coastal positions had to be very skilled. Cannons on land were heavier and more powerful than those on ships. Although at this time sea cannons on Spanish galleons had a range of about 400m, most pirate ship cannons would have not have been able to fire that far.

AVERY'S CANNON ▶

The British pirate Henry Avery poses at the scene of his most impressive victory. He fought against the Moghul fleet off Bombay in 1695 and captured two ships. His ship, the *Fancy*, carried 46 guns, but the Moghul treasure ship *Gang-i-sawai* shown in the picture, had 62. Avery's gunners aimed to bring down the masts, spars and sails of their victims' ships rather than sink them.

◀ EASTERN GUNFIRE

In 1843 the British naval vessel HMS *Dido* patrolled the North Borneo coast on behalf of James Brooke, who was the British ruler of Sarawak. In the mid-1800s, European interest in south-east Asia led to an increase in trade and shipping. This meant rich pickings for the local pirates, who were known as dayaks. The British quest was to destroy the pirate bases and fleets of galleys called prahus. The naval crews transferred to prahus so that they could sail up the shallow rivers. South-east Asian pirates defended themselves with swivel guns (small mounted cannon), but these were not very effective when pitted against superior European fire power.

Cannon at the Ready

In battle, the ships would manoeuvre to bring the enemy within their field of fire. Firing each cannon was a skilled but exhausting and dangerous task that could keep half-a-dozen men busy. The gun was run in and out of the gunport on a wheeled mounting, and was tightly secured by ropes. These secured the gun when it recoiled from the shot, flying backwards. Iron cannons were used in Europe by the 1300s, and the Europeans soon overtook the Chinese in the development of firearms. By the 1500s, even pirates were master gunners, and their ships were large enough to carry cannon.

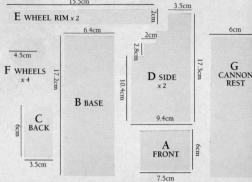

E WHEEL RIM x 2 — 15.5cm
F WHEELS x 4 — 4.5cm, 17.2cm
C BACK — 6cm, 3.5cm
B BASE — 6.4cm, 10.4cm
D SIDE x 2 — 2cm, 2.8cm, 17.3cm, 9.4cm
A FRONT — 6cm, 7.5cm
G CANNON REST — 3.5cm, 6cm, 17.3cm

1. Copy the templates, following the measurements shown above. Use thick card for all of them apart from the wheel and wheel rim templates, which should be on thin card. Cut all the templates out.

You will need: *30 x 30cm piece of stiff card, 15 x 15cm piece of thin card, pencil, ruler, scissors, wood glue, thick and thin paintbrushes, red and black paint, pair of compasses, 12.5 x 2cm strip of corrugated card, masking tape, 2 cardboard tubes about 13cm long, one 4cm diameter, one 3cm diameter, self-hardening clay, knitting needle or bradawl, 9cm length of ½cm-diameter dowel, kebab stick.*

6. Take the thinner of the two cardboard tubes. Wrap the 12.5 x 5cm strip of corrugated cardboard around one end. Secure with masking tape.

7. Glue the outer edge of the corrugated card ring. Insert the thinner cardboard tube into the wider cardboard tube to make the muzzle of the cannon.

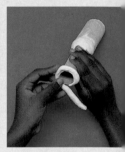

8. Cover the join between the inner and outer tubes by gluing on a strip of clay. Glue a thin roll of clay to the rim of th cannon's mouth and leave to dr

On board ship, cannon were often mounted on wheeled carriages, like this 32-pounder of the 1700s. The gunpowder was rammed down the barrel of the cannon. The more firmly it was packed, the more effective the explosion. A smouldering fuse set off the gunpowder charge with an almighty crash, and the shot hurtled toward its target. If the cannon balls burst into the hull or decks of a wooden ship, the impact caused a lethal shower of giant splinters. More deaths were caused by splinters than by the shot itself.

11. Pierce holes through th centre of each wheel with the knitting needle or bradawl. Be careful not to break them as they are quite delicate.

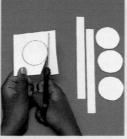

Glue the two sides **D** to **B**. Add end pieces **A** and **C**. Push inside so it's slightly lower than semi-circles on **D**. Let each ...tion dry before adding the next.

3 Use the thick paintbrush to paint the cannon base in one or two coats of bright red acrylic paint. Let the first coat dry before you apply the second.

4 Use a pair of compasses to draw the 4.5cm-diameter wheel sections on the thin card. Draw four wheel sections altogether, then cut them out.

5 Glue the two strips of card **E** around two of the circles. Glue the other two circles on top of the rim to make the drum-like wheels. Paint the wheels black.

Make two holes through the narrow barrel with the ...dawl. Enlarge them with the ...ndle of a paintbrush. Insert the ...wel and glue in place.

10 Use the thick paintbrush to paint the cannon and dowel with black paint. Allow the first coat to dry before applying a second coat.

A real cannon is described by the weight of the shot it can fire. The biggest guns on the largest naval warships of the 1700s were 32-pounders (23kg). Most guns on a pirate ship would be much smaller. Remember that your cannon is not made of metal. It will make an impressive display item in your room, but you should not try to fire it or play with matches.

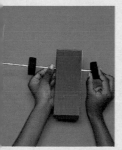

...2 Pierce the cannon base ...towards the front end ...th the kebab stick. Feed the ...ck through both holes. Put the ...eels on the stick as shown.

13 Cut the kebab stick to the right length, leaving ¾cm poking out beyond the wheels. Put a blob of clay on the ends to keep the wheels in place.

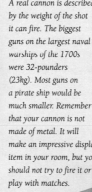

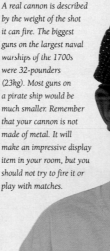

Pirate Treasure

Like any modern robbers, pirates throughout history wanted to win treasure that was valuable, easily transported and readily sold. Gold, silver and precious stones were always their first choice, either in the form of coins, ingots, jewellery, tableware or crosses stolen from churches. Vikings would even steal church bells and melt down the metal. Fine quality cloths, such as silks and heavy embroidered materials were always worth taking, and so was ivory. Sam Bellamy's *Whydah*, wrecked in a storm off Cape Cod, Massachusetts, in 1717, was discovered in 1983. The ship carried pieces-of-eight, gold bars and West African jewellery.

Many pirates' prizes were not at all glamorous, such as saltfish, hides, rare dyes, tobacco, spices or loaves (solid blocks) of sugar. Bulk cargoes were sometimes unwelcome because they were difficult to unload and sell without attracting attention. Equipment and supplies were always in demand, and captured ships were often stripped of weapons, charts, instruments, flags, tools, sailcloth, ropes, food and drink.

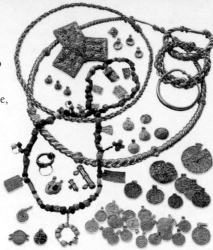

▲ VIKING HOARD

A hoard of Viking treasure reflects the wide area over which the warrior fleets raided and traded. It includes gold, silver and jewellery from the Anglo-Saxons and Franks of northern Europe. There are treasures, too, from the markets of Byzantium (modern Istanbul) and Baghdad. This hoard was buried at Hon in Norway in the AD860s to keep it safe from thieves.

◄ INCA GOLD

Solid gold figures were among treasures seized by Spanish invaders in the 1500s. The Spanish conquered many lands in Central and South America. They stripped the temples and palaces of the mighty Inca and Aztec empires of their gold. The native people were put to work in the silver mines of the Andes mountains. Soon mule trains were carrying untold riches to the Caribbean ports. The treasure ships that took the plunder to Spain were a prime target for pirates.

BARBARY PLUNDER ►

The Barbary corsairs often robbed treasure ships, even though their chief aim was to seize Christians as slaves. Many ships sailing from Venice, Genoa and Spain were laden with precious cargoes. In those days, money and treasure was transported in chests from one country to another – there were no simple bank transfers as there are today.

◄ FACT OR FICTION?

Did pirates really bury their treasure, as shown in this illustration from the 1700s? There have always been rumours and local tales of hidden plunder. Some pirates may have hidden their ill-gotten gains, never to return. However, little pirate treasure has ever been found. What has been discovered is treasure hidden *from* pirates – by nervous monks or merchants expecting a raid. Pirates usually sold on their treasure. Objects from temples and churches were often melted down into gold or silver bars first.

▲ SURGEON'S CHEST

Medical supplies may not be our idea of treasure, but to pirates they were very precious indeed. They could make the difference between life and death. In 1718 Blackbeard threatened to murder hostages and set the North American port of Charleston ablaze if a valuable medicine chest was not sent out to his ship at once. As usual, his demands were met.

◄ TREASURE TROVE

In 1927, a hoard of gold and silver was discovered in the Church of San José in Panama. Had the treasure been hidden by anxious priests or townsfolk, or was the church used during looting by buccaneers? The treasure was believed to date from 1671, when the city was sacked by the Welsh pirate Henry Morgan. It took 175 mules to carry the gold and silver coins, jewellery, precious gemstones, silks and spices they had ransomed from their prisoners.

▲ EQUAL SHARES

A democratic pirate crew shares out the spoils. By the 1720s, the readiness of pirates to cheat and trick each other had become such a problem that rules were drawn up and agreed before a voyage began. Captain George Lowther's pirates agreed to split the loot into shares, with each crew member receiving one share, the captain two shares, the ship's master 1½ shares and the doctor, first mate, gunner and boatswain 1¼ shares each.

A Dead Man's Chest

Fifteen men on the dead man's chest –
Yo-ho-ho, and a bottle of rum!
Drink and the devil have done for the rest....

The song is from the classic pirate story *Treasure Island* written by Robert Louis Stevenson in 1881. Both song and book conjured up the image of pirates burying chests of treasure and drawing up secret maps. In reality this rarely happened. However, sea chests were used as early as Viking times for carrying a sailor's personal possessions and weapons. The strongest chests, fitted with iron bands and locks, were used to store gold, silver and other treasure on board ship.

You will need: 50x 50cm corrugated cardboard, ruler, pencil, scissors, masking tape, cup of flour, about ½ cup of water, mixing bowl, fork, newspaper, fine sandpaper, brown acrylic paint, 5cm paintbrush, 25cm² black paper, white pencil, glue, matte wood varnish, 15 x 3cm black fabric.
Pieces of eight: self-hardening clay, cocktail stick or meat skewer, gold and silver paints.

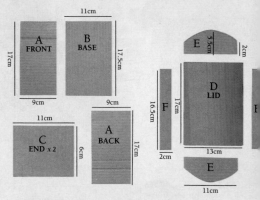

1 Copy the templates on to the cardboard, carefully following the measurements shown above. Cut them out.

When William Kidd returned to North America in 1699, he was said to be carrying £400,000-worth of plunder. He soon realized that he was going to be arrested for piracy, so he deposited shares of this treasure with friends. Eleven bags of silver and gold were left on Gardiner's Island, off Long Island, New York. The hoard was handed in to the authorities before Kidd's trial. There may be more still to be discovered. Teams have searched in Canada, others in Florida and the Caribbean – but none has ever been found.

4 Place the flour in a bowl, and add water gradually, a spoon at a time. Mix as you go, to make a smooth, thick paste rather like pancake batter.

5 Tear the newspaper into strips and coat each strip with the paste. Cover the chest and lid, inside and out, with three layers of these strips.

9 Glue on the corner reinforcements. Glue the bands on the sides and bottom of the chest. Space them evenly and match them up with each other.

10 Glue the bands on the lid. Make sure you match up and continue the patterns th are on the sides and base of the chest. Varnish the chest and lid.

2 Use the masking tape to join the side sections **A** and **C** to each other and to the base **B** to make a box shape. Tape along the inside joins as well.

3 Tape together the lid sides **E** and **F** (there are two of each). Bend the top **D** to fit the curve of the lid and tape in place. Tape along all the inside joins of the lid.

PIECES OF EIGHT

1 Mould the clay into ball shapes in the palms of your hands. Squash the balls into flat circles.

2 Look at real coins, or pictures of old coins. Engrave your coin designs with the cocktail stick.

3 Leave to harden and dry completely in a warm place. Then paint the coins gold and silver.

6 Leave for several hours in a warm, dry place. When the surfaces are completely hard and dry, rub them down with fine sandpaper until smooth.

7 Paint the chest and lid, inside and out, with one or two coats of brown acrylic paint. Leave the first coat to dry before you apply the second coat.

8 Use the white pencil to draw the iron bands and corners on the black paper. Use a ruler to measure the strips to the same size as the chest. Cut them out.

11 Take the black fabric strip and glue one half of it on to the inside back edge of the lid. It should be about half way along the lid edge.

12 Line up the lid and chest. Glue the other half of the fabric strip on to the inside back edge of the lower part of the chest to make a hinge.

You could line your chest with velvet to use as a money box or for your personal treasures. Pirate money would have been real gold and silver, such as the Spanish gold escudos (or doubloons) and the silver pesos of 8 reales (pieces-of-eight).

Piratical Punishments

Some pirates carried out sickening acts of cruelty against their victims and may even have enjoyed doing so. Torture, burning and mutilation were common. Chinese pirates kept their captives in cramped bamboo cages, or nailed them to the deck. Such atrocities were more than mere punishments. They might be a quick way of extracting information about where gold was hidden, and they were certainly useful for spreading terror among future victims. Life at sea was tough, even on official naval ships. Any pirate who disobeyed ship's rules or quarrelled with his shipmates faced flogging, beating or being set adrift in a small boat. If a pirate robbed another member of the crew, he might be punished by having his ears and nose slit. The crew of John Phillips, captain of the *Revenge* around 1720, had to swear (over an axe rather than a Bible) that deserters and traitors would be marooned. This involved being set ashore and abandoned on a remote island with one flask of gunpowder, a pistol, ammunition and just one bottle of water – enough to last no more than a day or two.

▲ HOMESPUN PUNISHMENT

A person about to be punished had to make a cat o' nine tails before being flogged with it. Rope was unwound and knotted at the ends. The cat may have been used by pirates to give captured officers a taste of their own medicine.

◀ REVENGE

Pirates seize the arm of a ship's captain and hack it off. Many pirates who had served their time on merchant ships or in the Navy had bitter memories of ill treatment by officers. When they captured ships, they often sought revenge on the officers by torturing them.

TOO KIND BY HALF ▶

The Irish pirate captain Edward England was punished by his crew for being too kindhearted. England's pirates were a constant threat to the great trading vessels of the East India Company. He is pictured here in front of the *Cassandra*, a ship he seized in the Comoro Islands in 1720. England gave the crew of the *Cassandra* the badly damaged pirate ship in exchange. The pirate crew was so furious at this act of mercy that they set England and his supporters adrift in a small boat. The men just managed to row across the Mozambique Channel to the island of Madagascar, where England soon died in poverty.

HUMAN SHOT ►

French citizens of Algiers become ammunition in this gruesome illustration. Algiers was a corsair stronghold on the Barbary coast. European warships blockaded the port several times during the 1800s. In revenge, the Muslim defenders are said to have fired living French people at the enemy ships. Over the centuries, terrible tales were told of Barbary cruelty. Many of them were probably exaggerated. Even so, both sides did torture and abuse their prisoners and slaves.

▲ ROASTED ALIVE

An English sea captain is tortured over burning coals in India. Piracy was common along India's west coast to the south of Bombay. This scene may be meant to show Khanhoji Angria or his sons in the 1700s. These pirates from the Maratha states fought a bitter war against European shipping, demanding the right to control the region's trade. Their claim was fair, but they were dismissed as common pirates.

UNSTEADY WALK ►

Pirates of the 1700s force a captive to walk the plank and fall into the sea, to drown or be eaten by sharks. Pirates did sometimes throw their victims overboard, but walking the plank seems to have been rare. The only known report of it happening is from a newspaper dated 1829.

Pirate Havens

Pirates have always needed bases, places where they could safely take on supplies and plan their next voyage. These havens needed to be easily defended and beyond the reach of the law. In the 1720s, the Welsh pirate captain Bartholomew Roberts and his crew holed up at a pirate colony in Sierra Leone, West Africa. It was run by a buccaneer called John Leadstone, or Old Crackers.

Sometimes pirates formed their own states, like miniature countries. On the shores of the Mediterranean Sea, there were entire colonies, founded by Greeks after about 700BC, that lived by piracy. Pirates who settled on the island of Madagascar off the East African coast about 300 years ago appointed themselves kings of the lands they seized.

The port of St Malo, in Brittany (in north-west France), lived by the corsair trade for hundreds of years. In the 1630s, the island of Tortuga, off Hispaniola in the Caribbean, was the chief base of the Caribbean buccaneers. Port Royal in Jamaica was another glory hole for pirates from the 1660s to the 1680s. It was followed a few years later by Nassau, in the Bahamas.

▲ A Promised Land?

A pictorial map shows the luxuriant setting of a pirate stronghold on the African island of Madagascar. From the 1690s to the 1720s, thousands of pirates from Europe and the Americas settled here. It was said to be warm all the time, to have beautiful women and plentiful food. The island paradise was shortlived though, for naval patrols were soon rounding the Cape of Good Hope in pursuit of the pirates.

City of the Corsairs ▼

In 1762, an English fleet attacked the port of St Malo on the north coast of France, tired of falling prey to privateers. The people of St Malo made fortunes by encouraging privateering and demanding payment from English and Dutch shipping as it headed up the English Channel. The most famous privateer was René Du Guay-Trouin (1673-1736), who became a French naval commander.

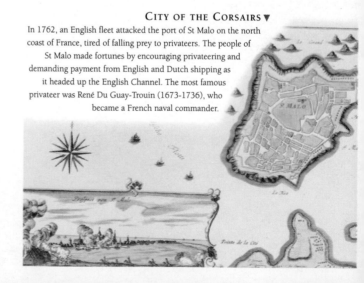

▲ Safe Harbour

Lower the mainsail, cast the anchor! A battle-weary pirate crew sails into harbour to rest and re-stock. The place is perfect, with a cove hidden by craggy cliffs and a narrow entrance difficult for unwanted visitors to navigate. The hills are rich in vegetation. There will be lots of fresh fruit to pick, and wild animals and birds to hunt.

◀ DRINK AND THE DEVIL

A pirate crew unwinds after several months at sea. Pirates were known for drinking too much alcohol such as wine, rum, gin and ale. They gambled too, playing at dice and cards, or placing bets on cockfights – to the death. Folk dances on the Atlantic coast of Nicaragua are said to have first been brought to the region by English pirates.

PIRATE KINGDOMS ▶

It was easy for pirates to lord it over local people who lived on the island of Madagascar in the 1600s. Some of the pirates set up their own kingdoms. One of them was Abraham Samuel, a Jamaican of mixed descent. He ruled a patch of land in the south of the island at Fort Dauphin (modern Tôlanaro) in the 1690s. Another settlement was the self-styled kingdom of the pirate James Plantain, in the north of the island. Plantain called himself the King of Ranter Bay.

◀ JAMAICA RETREAT

A peaceful view of Port Royal, Jamaica, gives little idea of the port's rowdy taverns and slave markets. The British captured Jamaica from the Spanish in 1655. At first, buccaneers were allowed to use the port – provided they continued to attack Spanish ships. However, by the 1690s the colonial governors had had enough and set about eliminating the pirate menace. Port Royal (near modern-day Kingston), was destroyed by an earthquake in 1692.

Brought to Justice

In about 470BC, magistrates in the Greek city of Teos had to declare three times a year that anyone found guilty of piracy, plunder or trading with pirates would be killed, along with their families. In Roman times, pirates were nailed to wooden crosses and left to die. Between AD1000 and 1500, in the German port of Hamburg, hundreds of pirates were beheaded by sword. In the 1600s and 1700s, the bodies of hanged pirates were left in chains where they could be easily seen, on the sandy shores of Jamaica and the mudflats of the River Thames, as a warning to all.

In the end, it was modern technology rather than fear of punishment that brought most pirates to justice. Fast steamships, powerful guns and, eventually, radio communication left pirates with nowhere to hide. By the 1930s, piracy had become very rare.

Then, in the 1980s, piracy made a comeback, often under the new name of hijacking. Luxury yachts were attacked in the Caribbean and off Greece. In south-east Asia, large oil tankers were boarded by robbers armed with modern guns. The new pirates now had radio, firepower and fast boats. The details were different, but it was an ancient story.

▲ Awaiting their Fate
No mercy is given and none is expected by pirates on trial. In the 1700s, new courts were set up to try pirates in Britain's American colonies. Naval officers and colonial governors passed judgment. Punishment was swift and merciless.

Death in London ▶
The body of a pirate is dragged through the streets, to be hacked apart and publicly burned. William de Marisco (or Marsh) was based on Lundy Island in the Bristol Channel off south-west England. He attacked ships all along the west coast until 1242, when he was captured, imprisoned in the Tower of London and then hanged.

End of a Pirate Squadron ▶
A Chinese pirate fleet was destroyed at Bias Bay, near Hong Kong, in September 1849. It was bombarded by a British naval force, and 400 pirates were killed. Pirate junks were destroyed on shore and piles of weapons were captured. The pirate chief, Cui A-Bao escaped justice, but only for a year or two. British efforts to stamp out piracy during the 1840s resulted in the deaths of over 2,000 pirates.

HANGED BY THE NECK ▶

Major Stede Bonnet, a plantation owner turned pirate, is hanged at Charleston, North America. He died on November 1718, together with 28 of his young crew. Bonnet had sailed with Blackbeard – and been cheated by him. He then operated along the coast of Virginia until he was caught. Colonial authorities in the Americas began clamping down on piracy in North American and Caribbean waters at the end of the 1600s. They placed bounties on pirates' heads as an incentive to capture them.

▲ THE DEATH MASK

A Chang Jiang River pirate gains immortality in this model cast from his head. Hundreds of Chinese pirates were beheaded in the 1800s. The executions were ordered by the Chinese Government and the European powers who governed some Chinese towns at that time. It was a brutal punishment, but one that the pirates had often practised on their own victims.

END OF AN AGE ▶

A group of Chinese pirates is beheaded at Kowloon in 1891. The last major period of piracy, based around the China Sea, was drawing to an end. Many of the pirates at that time were political rebels against both the Chinese Government and the foreign powers.

Timeline

There have been pirates as long as there have been trading ships to rob. The great age of piracy was during the 1600s and 1700s. It was a time when adventurers and explorers from Europe stormed their way around the world, greedy for treasure and power. Piracy became less common after the 1800s, but does still take place today.

700–100BC

565 GREEKS settle on the island of Corsica in the Mediterranean Sea and live by piracy.

532 POLYKRATES comes to power on the Greek island of Samos and turns to piracy, robbing friend and foe alike.

330 ALEXANDER THE GREAT tries to put an end to piracy in the Mediterranean – without a great deal of success.

Alexander the Great

Alexander the Great tackles Greek pirates

99BC–AD699

60BC THE ROMAN EMPEROR POMP[E] launches a 3-month campaign [to] end Mediterranean piracy. Te[n] thousand pirates are killed.

350s SHAPUR, RULER OF PERSIA tries to rid the Persian Gulf of pirates.

450s PRINCESS ALWILDA OF GOTLAND terrorizes the coast [of] the Baltic Sea.

450s IRISH PIRATES raid western British Isles.

Princess Alwilda

1500–1520s

1504 BARBARY CORSAIRS, under the Barbarossa brothers, capture papal treasure galleys in the Mediterranean.

1511 SCOTTISH PRIVATEER Andrew Barton plunders shipping off the coast of Flanders.

1522 GENOESE SEA CAPTAIN VERRAZANO, in French service, attacks a Spanish treasure fleet returning from the New World.

1523 ATTACK ON A SPANISH TREASURE FLEET returning from the New World, by French privateer Jean Fleury off Portugal.

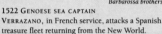
Barbarossa brothers

1530–1550s

1545 ROBERT RENEGER, seafarer from Southampton, England, captures the Spanish treasure galleon San Salvador off Portugal.

1553 FRENCH PRIVATEER, FRANÇOIS LE CLERC, often known as Jambe de Bois (wooden leg) attacks the Spanish.

1553 THE TURKISH CORSAIRS Dragut and Sinan occupy Tripoli (Libya).

1558 THOMAS STUCLEY, a noble-born rogue from Devon, England, is accused of piracy.

Spanish treasure ships attacked

1560s

1560-85 GRAINNE NI MHAILLE (GRACE O'MALLEY) runs a pirate fleet on Ireland's Atlantic coast.

1562 ENGLISH PRIVATEER JOHN HAWKINS starts trading slaves between West Africa and the Caribbea[n]

1568–72 CHANNEL PRIVATEERING by English, Frenc[h] and Dutch reaches its peak.

1569 DUTCH PRIVATEERS called the Sea Beggars start a campaign against Spanish ships and troops in the Netherlands.

Privateering in the English Channel

1660s & 70s

1660s BUCCANEERS attack Spanish treasure fleets in the Caribbean. Maltese corsairs attack Muslim fleets in the Mediterranean.

1668 WELSH PIRATE HENRY MORGAN leads buccaneer army into Puerto del Principe, on Spanish Cuba.

1674 HENRY MORGAN becomes the Lieutenant Governor of Jamaica.

1678 ALEXANDRE EXQUEMELIN, French surgeon and buccaneer, writes *Bucaniers of America.*

Jamaican rum

1680s

1680 BUCCANEER BARTHOLOMEW SHARP leads a plundering voyage around South America.

1681 LANCELOT BLACKBURNE, an English priest, keeps company with the Caribbean buccaneers. He later becomes Archbishop of York.

1688 HENRY MORGAN dies of drink.

1689 WILLIAM KIDD first serves as a privateer captain, in the Caribbean.

1689 MADAGASCAR becomes pirate haven, under pirate King Abraham Samuel.

Feasting in Madagascar

1690s

1690 THE PIRATE ROUND – from the Americas to the Indian Ocean via Africa – is established.

1692 PORT ROYAL, Jamaica, favourite haunt of buccaneers and pirates, is destroyed by an earthquake.

1693 AMERICAN PIRATE THOMAS TEW leaves Bermuda for the Indian Ocean.

1694 JEAN BART, a corsair from Dunkirk, is captured by the English – and escapes.

John Bart

1730–99

1736 DEATH OF FRENCH PRIVATEER René Duguay-Trouin, a St Malo corsair.

1756 FINAL DEFEAT of Maratha pirates in India.

1779 AMERICAN COLONIAL PRIVATEERS, such as Paul Jones, attack British shipping.

1795 FRENCH PRIVATEER ROBERT SURCOUF of St Malo attacks British shipping in the Indian Ocean.

Indian pirate torture

1800-1810

1803 AMERICAN FLEET makes an attack on Barbary pirates.

1807-10 QING ER SOU (MADAM CHENG) takes control of a vast pirate fleet in the South China Sea following her husband's death.

Qing Er Sou leads attack

1809 BRITISH FLEET DESTROYS PIRATE BASE at Ras al Khaima in the Persian Gulf.

1810 FRENCH PIRATE JEAN LAFITTE attacks ships sailing out of New Orleans in the southern states of North America.

1810s

1812 JEAN LAFITTE becomes an official privatee[r] in the service of America.

1816 ANGLO-DUTCH FLEET bombards Algiers to oust Barbary corsairs.

1819 ANTI-PIRACY TASK FORCE destroys pirate bases in the Persian Gulf.

Prisoners shot from Barbary mortars

D700–1010

9 Viking pirates begin to raid coastal settlements the British Isles.

46 Viking leader Ragnar Lodbrok besieges Paris.

59 Viking warrior Bjorn Ironside sails for the editerranean in search of plunder.

0–914 Vikings threaten onstantinople (modern anbul).

85 A Viking army attacks e city of Paris.

009 Viking Olaf the Stout pulls own London Bridge.

Olaf the Stout

1200s

1217 Flemish-born Eustace the Black Monk is beheaded in a sea battle off Sandwich, England.

1242 William de Marisco (Marsh) of Lundy Island is captured, hanged, quartered and burned in London.

1243 Early example of letter of marque is issued by King Henry III of England.

1281 Kublai Khan, Mongol emperor of China, launches unsuccessful attacks on Japan in response to Japanese piracy.

William de Marisco

1300–1499

1394 Harry Pay, sailing out of Poole, England, sacks the Spanish port of Gijon.

1399 Privateer John Hawley of Dartmouth, England, captures 34 vessels sailing from Normandy and Brittany.

1402 Störtebeker leader of the Baltic pirate band, the Friends of God and Enemies of the World, is executed in Germany.

1406 Harry Pay escapes the French and attacks ships in the River Seine.

Spanish treasure

1492 First voyage of Christopher Columbus, in the service of Spain, across Atlantic to the W Indies.

570s & 80s

572 English seafarer Francis Drake attacks panish at Nombre de Dios, a port on the Isthmus Panama.

573 Thirty-three German pirates and their leader lein Henszlein are executed in Hamburg, Germany.

578 Francis Drake raids Spain's Pacific ports.

580 John Oxenham, Drake's Lieutenant, is captured y the Spanish and hanged for piracy.

582 Lady Mary Killigrew leads Cornish pirates gainst a Spanish ship that is taking refuge from orms in Falmouth.

586 Francis Drake attacks Spanish at Cartagena in olombia, South America.

1600s & 1610s

1601 Uskok pirates from Segna, near Fiume (modern Rijeka in Croatia), attack Venetian shipping.

1607 English nobleman Sir Francis Verney joins the Muslim Barbary corsairs.

1611 Dutch pirate Simon Danziger, also known as Captain Devil, is hanged at Tunis, North Africa, after becoming a Barbary corsair and then rejoining the Christians.

1612 The English pirate Peter Easton leads a large pirate fleet to the Mediterranean to plunder merchant shipping.

Mediterranean corsair

1620s–50s

1620 Pirate republic is declared at Sallee, a territory on the Atlantic coast of Morocco.

1627 Dutch privateer Jan Jansz joins the Barbary corsairs and leads a slave raid on Iceland.

1630 The island of Tortuga in the Caribbean becomes a buccaneer base.

1642 Captain William Jackson, English privateer, signs up 1,000 men to plunder the Spanish Main.

1650 Major Spanish offensive against camps of British buccaneers.

.700–1709

700 The First ecord of a lack Jack ith skull- nd-crossbones eing flown.

701 Captain idd hanged in ondon for piracy.

705 Thomas Green, pirate captain, and 6 of his crew hanged in Edinburgh, Scotland.

Calico Jack's black jack flag

Blackbeard

1710s

1716-18 New Providence Bahamas, is established as a major pirate base.

1717 The pirate ship Whydah, commanded by Sam Bellamy, is wrecked on the coast of Cape Cod, America.

1718 Major Stede Bonnet, plantation owner turned pirate, is hanged. Edward Teach (Blackbeard) is killed.

1718 Christopher Condent attacks shipping off Africa and Arabia.

1719 Howell Davis, Welsh pirate, dies on Africa's Guinea Coast. Bartholomew Roberts, Welsh pirate, leads devastating attacks on Guinea coast.

1720s

1720 Mary Read and Anne Bonny are brought to trial in Jamaica. Their associate, Calico Jack Rackham, is hanged. Pirate Charles Vane is hanged in Jamaica.

1720s Pirate James Plantain declares himself king of Ranter Bay, Madagasar.

1722 Bartholomew Roberts' pirate crew captured in Africa, 52 hanged. Mathew Luke's pirate crew tried in Jamaica, 41 hanged.

1723 Thomas Anstis Pirate captain is murdered in Caribbean by his own crew.

Mary Read

820s–40s

826 Rahmah bin Jabr, n Arab pirate, aged 70, lows up his own ship n battle.

827 Benito de Soto, Spanish pirate, attacks tlantic shipping.

843 British begin campaign gainst Dayak pirate bases in orneo and Sulu Sea.

849 British destroy Chinese irate fleet off the Vietnam coast.

Chinese pirate beheads his victim

1850s–60s

1851 Cui A-Bao, lieutenant of Chinese pirate chief Shi Wu-Zai, kills himself in jail.

1843 British begin campaign against Dayak pirate bases in Borneo and Sulu Sea.

1849 British destroy the last Chinese pirate fleet off the coast of Vietnam.

1836 Privateering abolished by Britain, France and Russia.

1857 Eli Boggs, an American pirate, is captured in the South China Sea by American merchant captain and rogue Henry Hayes.

pirate junk

1900s

airline hijacked

oil tanker attacked

a1920s–30s Last days of Chinese piracy as political rebels take to the sea.

1985 Achille Lauro, an Italian cruise liner is hijacked by Palestinian terrorists.

1992 The British Navy in South-east Asia launches piracy patrol after supertanker is attacked by pirates.

GLOSSARY

Barbary Coast
A section of the North African coast famed for its corsairs (from Berbers, the people of the region).

becalmed
The state of a sailing ship when it cannot move because there is no wind.

bilge
The lowest section of a ship's hull.

blackjack
A black pirate flag.

boom
The spar to which a sail is attached so that it can be moved according to wind direction.

bow
The front, pointed part of a ship.

bowsprit
A long spar projecting from a ship's prow.

brigantine
A two-masted sailing ship, square-rigged on both masts, with a fore-and-aft sail on the lower part of the mainmast.

buccaneers
Pirates and privateers who plundered Spanish ships and treasure ports in the West Indies and Central America in the 1600s.

calico
A type of cotton cloth, either white or boldly patterned.

capstan
Winding gear, used for raising anchors or sails.

careen
To beach a ship, so its hull can be cleaned and repaired.

caulk
To seal leaking ship's timbers with fibre and pitch (tar).

corsair
(1) A pirate or a privateer, especially in the Mediterranean region and northern France.
(2) The ship sailed by (1).

crow's nest
A small platform high up on a mast, which is used as a lookout position.

cutlass
A slashing sword used by sailors from the 1600s onwards.

dhow
An Arab sailing ship with one or two masts and triangular sails.

draught
The depth of the ship below water, which is also the maximum depth of water it can float in.

East Indiaman
A large English or Dutch merchant vessel that traded with Asia.

ensign
A flag flown from the stern of a ship.

figurehead
A decorative wooden figure found on the prow of some sailing ships.

filibuster
A French buccaneer.

flintlock pistol
An early type of pistol in which a piece of flint is made to spark and set off the gunpowder.

fo'c'sle
An abbreviation of forecastle, the raised deck at the front of a ship.

fore-and-aft
Having sails that are lined up with the length of the ship (the opposite of square-rigged).

furl
Gathering in and folding up a sail.

fuse
A slow-burning length of cord that is used to set off the charge in a cannon.

galleon
A big sailing ship with three or more masts, used from the 1500s to the 1700s as a warship and a Spanish treasure ship.

galley
(1) Any large ship powered by oars.
(2) A ship's kitchen.

grappling iron
Metal hooks attached to a long rope. They were thrown on to an enemy ship to help boarding.

Guinea Coast
The coast around the Gulf of Guinea (West Africa).

gunport
An opening in a ship's side through which a cannon was fired.

halyard
A rope used to hoist a flag or a sail.

hard tack
Ship's biscuits.

hourglass
A primitive instrument for telling the time, which uses sand running through a glass tube to indicate the passing of one hour.

hull
The main, outer body of a ship.

jack
A square flag flown from the front of a ship indicating nationality.

jib
A triangular sail that is set at the front of a ship between the foremast and bowsprit.

Jolly Roger
The common term for any pirate flag.

junk
(1) A wooden sailing ship commonly used in China and the Far East.
(2) Bits of old rope used for caulking.
(3) Salted meat.

landlubber
A person with little experience of life at sea.

letter of marque
A licence or certificate issued by a monarch or government, authorizing the bearer to attack enemy shipping.

log-book
A written record of a ship's voyage, noting course, speed and daily events.

longship
A long, streamlined wooden ship sailed by Viking raiders and explorers.

magazine
The place where gunpowder is stored on a ship.

Malouin
A person from the port of St Malo, in France.

marlinspike
A metal spike used to separate strands of rope.

maroon
To set someone ashore on a remote island, to abandon.

mizzen
The rear sail on a three-masted vessel.

musket
An early type of gun.

mutiny
To refuse to obey an officer's orders, or open revolt on board ship.

oakum
Old rope fibres, unpicked and used for caulking.

pennant
A triangular flag or streamer flown from a mast-top.

pieces of eight
Silver pesos (Spanish coins), which were worth eight reales.

piracy
Robbery at sea, stealing or destruction of ships, coastal raiding.

piragua
A small sailing canoe used by the early buccaneers in the Caribbean.

Pirate Round
A popular route taken by pirates from the 1690s onwards – North America or the Caribbean to West Africa, Madagascar, the Red Sea and then back across the Atlantic Ocean.

prahu
A type of wooden galley used in south-east Asia.

press
To force someone to join a ship's crew.

privateer
(1) Someone who is legally authorized to attack the ships of an enemy.
(2) The ship sailed by (1).

prow
The bow (front) of a ship.

ratlines
Cross-ropes on the shrouds, forming a rope ladder that enables the sailors to climb to the top of the mast.

renegade
Someone who changes sides, a turncoat or traitor.

sack
To raid or plunder, usually including robbery and destruction.

schooner
A small, fast sailing ship, which usually has two masts rigged fore-and-aft.

scurvy
A disease caused by a lack of Vitamin C in the diet. Symptoms include bleeding gums and spots.

sea-beggar
A member of a famous band of Dutch privateers.

shot
Ammunition of iron or lead that is fired from a musket or a cannon.

shrouds
Ropes running from the side of a ship to the top of its mast in order to support it.

sloop
A fast, small, single-masted sailing ship.

Spanish Main
(1) The Spanish-ruled mainland of Central and South America.
(2) The Caribbean region and the Gulf of Mexico.

spar
A wooden pole used for the mast or yard of a sailing vessel.

splice
To interweave two rope ends in order to join them.

spritsail
A sail hanging from a spar beneath the bowsprit.

square-rigged
Having square sails set at right angles to the mast (the opposite of fore-and-aft).

staff
(1) A pole on which a flag is hung.
(2) A length of wood marked with measurements used to calculate angles and distances in navigating.

stern
The back end of a ship.

topgallant
A sail above the topsail.

topsail
A sail above the mainsail or foresail.

yard
The spar (wooden pole) to which the top of a sail is attached.

INDEX